The
JEWISH
BOOK of
NUMBERS

The
JEWISH
BOOK of
NUMBERS

RONALD H. ISAACS

𝒜

JASON ARONSON INC.
Northvale, New Jersey
London

The author gratefully acknowledges permission to reprint from the following sources:

Weekly Torah portions are reprinted from *The How To Handbook for Jewish Living*, volume 1, by Kerry M. Olitzky and Ronald H. Isaacs. Copyright © 1993 by Kerry M. Olitzky and Ronald H. Isaacs. Published by Ktav Publishing House, Inc. Used by permission.

Population figures for cities and counties in the United States adapted from *The American Jewish Year Book*. Copyright © 1992 by the American Jewish Committee and the Jewish Publication Society. Used by permission.

This book was set in 12 pt. Garamond by Aerotype, Inc.

Library of Congress Cataloging-in-Publication Data

Isaacs, Ronald H.
    The Jewish book of numbers / Ronald H. Isaacs.
        p.   cm.
    Includes bibliographical references and index.
    ISBN 1-56821-951-2 (alk. paper)
    1. Judaism—Miscellanea. 2. Numbers in the Bible. 3. Lists in rabbinical literature. 4. Gematria. I. Title.
    BM582.I83 1996
    296—dc20
                                                    96-13669
                                                    CIP

Manufactured in the United States of America. Jason Aronson Inc. offers books and cassettes. For information and catalog write to Jason Aronson Inc., 230 Livingston Street, Northvale, New Jersey 07647.

Teach Us to Number Our Days

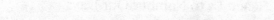

CONTENTS

INTRODUCTION

Ever since primitive people learned to count on their fingers, numbers have had a special significance. Among various peoples and religions, they have even assumed sacred proportions, some being considered lucky and others being unlucky. Numbers, lists, and summaries can play an important role in Jewish education. They can help separate and clarify the major points of a subject from among a mass of information.

The Jewish Bible is replete with numbers that were sometimes meant to be taken at face value, but more likely to be noteworthy for their symbolic nuances. With the advent of *gematriah* (the rabbinic methodology for explaining a word or words using the numerical value of Hebrew letters), we begin to see the use of Jewish numerology as commentary to explain various Jewish texts. This form of interpretation has been used both as a form of arithmetical amusement as well as a popular form of interpretation in the literature of the Kabbalah (Jewish mysticism). *Gematriah* has continued to be used today as one system of discovering the hidden meanings of all sorts of Jewish texts. The results of its use have been many novel and curious interpretations of both biblical and rabbinic texts. The accumulated Jewish folklore throughout the generations continues to make use of interpretive Jewish numerology and to express the importance of numbers in all phases of life.

It is the purpose of this volume to introduce readers to the amazing world of Jewish numbers, lists, and summaries. Included within the book are references to biblical arithmetic and methods of biblical numerical expression, examples of sacred numbers, Jewish units of time and measurement, numbered Jewish lists and summaries, noteable Jewish quotations that use numbers, and a section on *gematriah*.

May you find much pleasure in learning about Jewish numerology. It is my hope that this volume will stimulate you toward further study!

BIBLICAL NUMBERS

Biblical numbers are primarily based on the decimal system, which is said to be of Hamito-Egyptian origin. The sexagesimal system, deriving from Sumerian usage, also plays an important part in the Bible, and since the number 60 is divisible by 10 and 5, the two methods easily combine one with the other.

Biblical numbers range from 1 (Genesis 1:5) to 100,000,000 (Daniel 7:10), though the number in Daniel is usually interpreted symbolically and not literally. One of the largest numbers that commentators consider to be nonsymbolic is that given in 1 Chronicles 21:5 in connection with the census taken by King David: he counted 1,100,000 men from Israel plus 470,000 from Judah who drew the sword. The idea of infinity in the mathematical sense does not appear in the Bible.

BIBLICAL ARITHMETIC

The Israelites during biblical times did not take any special interest in mathematics per se. Rather, they were interested in knowledge of arithmetic in order to conduct their lives' day-to-day routines.

Four basic arithmetical operations appear in the Bible, but only the results, not the methodology in the calculation. The following are examples of addition, subtraction, multiplication, and division, as exemplified in the Bible.

Addition

In this example (Numbers 11:26), two men (Eldad and Medad) of the seventy elders had remained within the camp. The verse reads: "But there remained *two* men in the camp, the name of the *one* was Eldad, and the name of the *one* Medad."

Subtraction

In this example (Genesis 18:28–33), Abraham challenges God's Divine justice as he pleads to God that the cities of Sodom and Gomorrah not be destroyed. The verses read:

And God said: "If I find in Sodom *50* righteous within the city, then I will forgive all the place for their sake." And Abraham answered and said: "Behold now, I have taken upon me to speak to God, who am but dust and ashes. If there shall lack *5* of the *50* righteous, will You destroy all of the city for lack of *5?*" And God said, "If I find there *40* and *5*, I will not destroy it." And he spoke unto God yet again, and said: "If there shall be *40* found there." And God said: "I will not do it for the *40*'s sake." And Abraham said: "Oh, let not God be angry, and I will speak. If there shall be *30* found there." And God said: "I will not do it if I find *30* there." And Abraham said: "If I shall find *20* there." And God said: "I will not destroy it for the sake of *20*." And Abraham said: "Oh, let not God be angry, and I will speak yet but this once. If *10* shall be found there." And God said: "I will not destroy it for the sake of *10*."

Multiplication

In this example (from Leviticus 25:8), God presents the concept of the Jubilee Year, the *fiftieth* year, in which Hebrew slaves and their families were to be emancipated and all property in a walled city returned to its original owner. The verse reads: "And you shall number *7* Sabbaths of years unto you, *7* times *7* years. And there shall be for you the days of *7* Sabbaths of years, even *40* and *9* years."

Division

In this example (from Numbers 31:27), there was stated the apportionment of the spoil for those who fought in war. Here is the verse: "Divide the prey into *2* parts, between the men skilled in war, that went out to battle, and all of the congregation."

FRACTIONS

The Bible on occasion also uses fractions. Here are several examples of their use.

In this example (2 Kings 11:7), the division of guards for the king is presented. Here is the verse: "*One-third* part of you that enters in on the Sabbath shall even be keeping watch in the king's house. And *one-third* part shall be at the gate of Sur, and *one-third* part shall keep watch at the house, as a defense. And *two parts* of you all that are relieved on the Sabbath, even they shall keep watch in the house of the Lord about the king."

In this example (Genesis 47:24), Joseph presents to the people the apportionment of the crops of the field. The verse states: "Then Joseph said to the people, 'Whereas I have this day acquired you and your land for Pharaoh, here is seed for you to sow the land. And when the harvest comes, you shall give *one-fifth* to Pharaoh, and *four-fifths* shall be yours as seed for the fields and as food for you.' "

In this verse (Nehemiah 11:1), the Jewish people cast lots to see who will live in Jerusalem and who in the other cities. The verse states: "And the rules of the people dwelled at Jerusalem, and the rest of the people cast lots to bring *one* of every *ten* to dwell in Jerusalem the holy city, and the *nine* parts to remain in the other cities."

USE OF BODY PARTS TO EXPRESS NUMBERS

It is especially interesting to note that on occasion, the Bible would use certain parts of the anatomy to express a fraction or the arithmetic operation of multiplication. Several examples follow.

Yad (Hand) (Genesis 43:34): Concerning Benjamin's portion of food, the Bible states: "Benjamin's portion was *five* times [in Hebrew, "five hands"] more than any of theirs."

Regel (Foot) (Numbers 22:28): In this example, regarding the number of times that Bilaam hit his donkey, the Bible states: "And God opened the mouth of the donkey and she said to Bilaam, 'What have I done to

you, that you have smitten me these *three* times [in
Hebrew, "three feet"]?' "

Rosh (Head): The word *rosh* is often used in the Bible
to mean the sum total. For example, in Exodus 30:12,
which discusses the law of the shekel and the census of
the warriors, the verse states: "When you take the sum
[Hebrew, *rosh*] of the children of Israel, according to
their number, then shall they give every man a ransom
for his soul to God."

BIBLICAL METHODS OF EXPRESSION

Biblical numbers are expressed by words denoting
units: 10; 100; 200; 1,000; 2,000; 10,000; 20,000; and
various combinations of these numbers. They are not
always intended to be taken literally, at face value, but
more often are used symbolically or figuratively. Sometimes the rhetorical effect of numbers becomes apparent when certain words or names occur in the Bible a
given number of times, although the actual numeral is
never specified. There are many numbers that are noteworthy for their symbolic nuances, and several numbers that repeat so many times in the Bible that they
were considered sacred. Here are the examples of the
prominent sacred numbers as they appear in the Bible,
in rabbinic writings, and in Jewish life in general, beginning with the number one.

THE NUMBER ONE

THE NUMBER ONE IN THE BIBLE

The number one is, on occasion, used in the Bible as an indefinite pronoun. For example, in 2 Kings 4:39 it states: "So *one* of them went out into the fields to gather sprouts." In this case, the number one refers to anyone, a certain person, who is not identified in the text.

The number one is also used in the Bible as an indefinite article. For instance, in the Book of 1 Samuel 24:14, it states: "After whom is the king of Israel gone out? After whom are you pursuing? After a dead dog, after a *single* flea?"

Though one is often used as a cardinal number, it is also used in the Bible as an ordinal as well. Here are a couple of examples of the use of one as an ordinal number.

And there was evening and there was morning, the *first* day. (Genesis 1:5)

The waters went on diminishing until the tenth month; in the tenth month, on the *first* day, the tops of the mountains became visible. (Genesis 8:5)

They married Moabite women, the *first* named Orpah and the other Ruth. (Ruth 1:4)

Finally, the number one can signify uniqueness and indivisibility in the Bible. For example, in Genesis 2:24, it is the expression par excellence of the unity of marriage: "Hence a man leaves his father and mother and clings to his wife, so that they become *one* flesh."

The number one is also expressive of the doctrine of monotheism and the idea of One God. This has its ultimate expression in the statement appearing in Deuteronomy 6:4, which has become the watchword of the Jewish People: "Hear, O Israel, the Lord our God, the Lord is *One.*"

THE NUMBER ONE IN RABBINIC THOUGHT

Here are some examples of the number one as it appears in rabbinic teaching.

1. "Rabbi Eliezer ben Jacob said: He who performs *one* precept acquires for himself *one* advocate; but he who commits *one* transgression acquires for himself *one* accuser" (*Ethics of the Fathers* 4:13).
2. "Better is *one* hour of repentance and good deeds in this world than the whole life of the World to Come. And better is *one* hour of bliss in the World to Come than the whole life of this world" (*Ethics of the Fathers* 4:22).
3. The Rabbis ask: "And now is not God *One?* What mean the words: 'In that day God shall be *One* and His Name shall be *One*'? The answer is: Now God is *One,* but His Names are many. Everyone conceives Him according to his own vision. But in the world that is to be—in that

glorious future that is yet to come—not only will God
be *One,* but His Name will be *One* also" (Talmud
Pesachim 50a).

4. "For the sake of *one* righteous man the whole world is
    preserved in existence, as it is written: 'The righteous
    man is an everlasting foundation [Proverbs 10:25]' "
    (Talmud *Yoma* 38b).

5. "A nonbeliever once asked Shammai to convert him,
    provided he could teach him the entire Torah while
    standing on *one* leg. Shammai, who was quite impatient,
    drove him away. When he approached Hillel with the
    same request, Hillel said: 'That which is hateful to you,
    do not do to your neighbor. This is the whole Law, the
    rest is its commentary' " (Talmud *Shabbat* 31a).

6. "Not *one* thing is created in vain by the Almighty. He
    created the snail as a remedy for a scab; the fly for the
    sting of a wasp; the gnat for the bite of a serpent; the
    serpent for healing the itch; the spider for the sting of
    the scorpion" (Talmud *Shabbat* 77b).

7. "Man was created singly, as an individual, to teach that
    he who destroys *one* soul is considered as if he had
    destroyed the entire world. He who preserves *one* soul
    is considered as though he had preserved the entire
    world. And further, for the sake of peace, so that no
    person can say: 'My father was greater than yours!' "
    (Talmud *Sanhedrin* 37a).

8. "The Almighty's greatness is evident in many things.
    An example is that with *one* die a man mints many
    coins and all are exactly alike. Whereas the Lord, with
    one die, impressed the same image of Adam on all men,
    yet not *one* of them is like his neighbor" (Talmud
    Sanhedrin 37a).

9. "The person who learns from his companion *one*
    chapter, *one halachah, one* verse, *one* expression, or

even *one* letter, should treat him with respect" (*Ethics of the Fathers* 6:2).

THE NUMBER ONE IN THE LITURGY

The number one continues to permeate Jewish liturgy, mostly as an expansion of the doctrine on monotheism and the idea of One God. Here are some examples from the prayer book of the use of the number one.

Peerless and *unique* [i.e., One alone] is God, with none to compare to Him. (Prayer *Adon Olam,* Eternal God)

Hear, O Israel, the Lord our God, the Lord is *One.* (Prayer *Shema Yisrael,* Hear, O Israel)

You have called us from all peoples and tongues, constantly drawing us near to You, that we may lovingly offer You praise, proclaiming Your *Oneness.* (Prayer *Ahava Rabbah*)

God shall be acknowledged King of all the earth. On that day God shall be *One* and God's Name shall be *One.* (Prayer *Aleynu*)

God is *One* and God's Name is *One.* (Prayer *Lecha Dodi*)

God is *One,* unique. (Prayer *Yigdal*)

One is our God, great our Lord, holiness is His nature. (Service for taking out the Torah)

One, who knows *one? One,* I know *one. One* is our God, who is in heaven and earth. (Song "*Echad Mi*

Yode'ah,'' "Who Knows One," from the Passover Haggadah)

The *one* kid, the *one* kid, that father bought for two zuzim, the *one* kid. (Song "*Chad Gadya,*" "One Kid," from the Passover Haggadah)

The Number Two

THE NUMBER TWO IN THE BIBLE

Since a variety of the organs and limbs of a human being occur in pairs of two (eyes, ears, hands, feet), it stands to reason that the number two would be given a certain degree of importance. Here are several examples from the Bible related to the appearance of the number two.

1. "They came to Noah into the ark, *two* of each of all flesh in which there was breath of life" (Genesis 7:15).

2. "When God finished speaking with Moses on Mount Sinai, God gave Moses the *two* tablets of the Pact, stone tablets inscribed with the finger of God" (Exodus 31:18).

3. "If, however, he is poor and his means are insufficient, he shall take . . . *two* turtledoves or *two* pigeons, depending on his means" (Leviticus 14:21–22).

4. "Joshua, son of Nun, secretly sent *two* spies from Shittim" (Joshua 2:1).

5. "And there will I meet with you, and I will speak with you from above the ark-cover, from between the *two* cherubim which are upon the ark of the covenant" (Exodus 16:22).

The fraction of one half is also common in the Bible. Here are several examples of this fraction.

1. "So Moses assigned to them—to the Gadites, the Reubenites, and the *half-tribe* of Manasseh son of Joseph" (Numbers 32:33).

2. "This is what everyone who is entered to the records shall pay: a *half-shekel* by the sanctuary weight as an offering to God" (Exodus 30:13).

THE NUMBER TWO IN RABBINIC THOUGHT

Here is a sampling of the number two as it appears in rabbinic teaching.

1. "Rabbi Chananiah ben Tradion said: If *two* sit together and no words of the Torah are spoken between them, they are a session of scoffers. . . . But if two sit together and the words of the Torah are spoken between them, the Divine Presence rests between them" (*Ethics of the Fathers* 3:3).

2. "*Two* types of impulse beat within a person: one brings health and the other disease. The stronger conquers" (*Tikkune Zohar* 151a).

3. "Man tends to God in *two* ways: by gifts to the poor and generosity on the Sabbath and Festivals" (*Zohar* II: 35a).

4. "*Two* creatures are blinded in man—one intended for this life, and the other for the life hereafter" (*Bereshit Rabbah* 8).

5. "In *two* ways does man lend to God: in donating to the needy and in spending money for the Sabbath and Festivals" (*Zohar* II:255a).

6. "*Two* types of garments were given to the soul: the body and the light of knowledge. The latter is called the garment of the Rabbanan" (*Zohar* I:264a).

7. "If *two* scholars living in one city do not agree concerning *halachah* [i.e., Jewish law], one dies and the other is exiled" (Talmud *Sotah* 49).

8. "The Almighty permitted man to create *two* things after Creation. One was fire, which through Divine inspiration Adam drew forth by striking *two* stones together; the other was the mule, which was produced by cross-breeding" (Talmud *Pesachim* 54a).

9. "If speech is worth one selah [coin], silence is worth *two*" (Talmud *Megillah* 18a).

10. "When *two* sit at one table, the senior of them puts forth his hand first, and then the junior; if the junior puts forth his hand first, he is a glutton" (Talmud *Derech Eretz Rabbah* 57a).

11. "Until the Temple was built, the world rested on a shaky throne with only *two* legs. After the Temple was built, the world stood firm, its well-being assured" (*Tanchuma Terumah* 9).

12. "I looked up again and saw *two* women come soaring with the wind in their wings—they had wings like those of a stork—and carry off the tub between earth and sky. 'Where are they taking the tub?' I asked the angel who talked with me. And he answered: 'To build a shrine for it in the land of Shinar [Zechariah 5:9–11].' " Rabbi Yochanan said in the name of Rabbi Simeon ben Yochai: "The *two* women symbolize hypocrisy and arrogance, which made their home in Babylon" (Talmud *Sanhedrin* 24a).

13. "Rabbi Simon said: Be'eri uttered only *two* verses
in prophecy, and since they were not sufficient to make
up a separate book, they were attached to the Book of
Isaiah. The *two* verses were 'And when they shall say
[Isaiah 8:19],' and the verse that follows it" (Midrash
Leviticus Rabbah 6:6).

THE NUMBER TWO IN JEWISH LIFE

The number two has played a fairly prominent role in
Jewish life. The following are some examples of well-
known *twos* in Jewish life.

1. "When the Jewish People accepted the words of
the Torah, they recited these [*two*] words: '*Na'aseh
ve'nishma*—We will do and obey' " (Exodus 24:7).

2. "There are two parts to the phylacteries (i.e.,
tefillin): the hand piece and the head piece. This is
based upon the verse 'You shall bind them as a sign
upon your hand, and they shall be for frontlets between
your eyes' " (Deuteronomy 6:8).

3. "The Ten Commandments, with some slight vari-
ation, are mentioned two times in the Bible. Once it is
mentioned in Exodus 20 and the other time in Deuteronomy" (5:7ff.).

4. "In order to testify effectively in a Jewish court of
law, called a *Bet Din*, two witnesses are required. This
law is based upon the following biblical verse: 'At the
mouth of two witnesses, or three witnesses, shall he
that is to die be put to death' " (Deuteronomy 8:6).

5. "The recitation of the blessing over the wine (the
Kiddush) on both the Sabbath and Jewish holidays is to
occur two times, one before the evening meal and the
second time before the afternoon meal."

THE NUMBER THREE

THE NUMBER THREE IN THE BIBLE

The number three is a fairly common one in the Bible. At times it is quite difficult to ascertain whether it is used with precision or simply as a small round number. For example, in Genesis 30:36, it states that Laban put a distance of *three* days' journey between himself and Jacob while Jacob was pasturing the rest of Laban's flock. In yet another example (Exodus 2:2), we learn that "the woman conceived and bore a son [i.e., Moses], and when she saw how beautiful he was, she hid him for *three* months." In both of these examples, one cannot be sure whether the number three is being used as an exact, concrete number or simply an approximation.

Of special importance is the use of the number three in sacred contexts, where it often conveys the notion of completeness, since it has a beginning, middle, and end. Even in ancient times the pagans worshipped triads of gods. For example, in Babylon the people worshipped the triad of Anu, Bel, and Ea, whereas in Egypt the triad of Isis, Osiris, and Horus was worshipped. The universe was divided into heaven, earth, and the netherworld, which the three deities were said to represent. The family group of father, mother, and child also undoubtedly contributed to the significance of the number three.

In the Bible the number three has various religious associations. Here are several examples of the number three as it is used with religious significance:

1. "When Abraham asked God how he would know that he possessed the land, God answered as follows: Bring me a *three*-year-old heifer, a *three*-year-old she-goat, a *three*-year-old ram, a turtledove, and a young bird" (Genesis 15:9).

2. "For *three* years the eating of the fruit of a newly planted tree was forbidden" (Leviticus 19:23).

3. "*Three* times a year you shall hold a Festival for Me. You shall observe the Feast of Unleavened Bread[,] . . . the Feast of the Harvest . . . and the Feast of the Ingathering" (Exodus 23:14).

4. We learn of ritual purification taking place on the third day in the following verse: "He shall cleanse himself with it on the *third* day" (Numbers 19:12).

5. In the Book of Daniel we learn of the custom of praying three times a day: "*Three* times every day he kneeled upon his knees and prayed" (Daniel 6:11).

6. In Genesis 40:10–13, the number three has symbolic significance. The chief of the butlers tells his dream to Joseph, and says, " 'In my dream a vine was before me. And on the vine were *three* branches, and it was as though it budded, shot forth its blossoms.' . . . And Joseph said to him, 'This is its interpretation. The

three branches are *three* days. Within *three* days will Pharaoh lift up his head and restore you to office.' ''

7. The number three exercises a mystical power in the story of the Prophet Elijah's revival of a child: ''Then he stretched out over the child *three* times, and cried to God saying, 'O God, let this child's life return to his body!' '' (1 Kings 17:21).

8. In Deuteronomy 19:7–9, three cities of refuge are mentioned: ''That is why I command you: set aside *three* cities. . . . If you faithfully observe all this instruction that I enjoin upon you this day, to love the Lord your God and to walk in all of His ways at all times—then you shall add *three* more towns to those *three*.''

9. The number three is latent in a number of biblical passages where it expresses a complete and perfect number or is used for emphasis. For example, the phrase ''and God blessed'' occurs three times in Genesis (1:22, 1:28, 2:3): God blessed them, saying, ''Be fertile and increase.'' God blessed them and said, ''Be fertile and increase, and fill the earth and master it.'' And God blessed the seventh day and declared it holy, because on it God stopped all of the work of creation that He had done.

10. In Aaron's blessing (Numbers 6:24–26), God's Name occurs three times and three pairs of blessings are pronounced: ''The Lord bless you and protect you. The Lord deal kindly with you and graciously with you. The Lord bestow His favor upon you and grant you peace.''

11. The number three in the Book of Isaiah (6:3) appears to be used as a form of a superlative: ''Holy,

holy is the Lord of Hosts, His Presence fills the entire earth.''

THE NUMBER THREE IN RABBINIC THOUGHT

The number three plays a fairly prominent role in the rabbinic writings. Here is a sample of the number three in rabbinic teaching.

1. "The Men of the Great Assembly said *three* things: Be deliberate in judgment, raise up many disciples, and make a fence around the Torah" (*Ethics of the Fathers* 1:1).

2. "Simon the Just used to say: By *three* things the world exists: by the Torah, by the Temple service, and by deeds of loving-kindness" (*Ethics of the Fathers* 1:2).

3. "Rabbi Simeon ben Gamliel said: By three *things* is the world sustained: by truth, by justice, and by peace" (*Ethics of the Fathers* 1:18).

4. "Consider *three* things and you will not fall into the power of transgression: know what is above you—a seeing eye and a hearing ear and all your deeds are written in a book" (*Ethics of the Fathers* 2:1).

5. "Akabya ben Machalalel said: Consider *three* things and you will not fall into the power of transgression. Know whence you came, whither you are going, and before whom you are about to give account and reckoning" (*Ethics of the Fathers* 3:1).

6. "Rabbi Simeon said: If *three* have eaten at one table and have not spoken over it words of Torah, it is as though they had eaten of the sacrifices of the dead. . . . But if *three* have eaten at one table and have spoken over

it words of Torah, it is as if they had eaten from the table of the All-Present" (*Ethics of the Fathers* 3:4).

7. "Rabbi Simeon said: There are *three* crowns—the crown of the Torah, the crown of priesthood, and the crown of kingship—but the crown of a good name excels them all" (*Ethics of the Fathers* 4:17).

8. "He who possesses these *three* qualities is of the disciples of Abraham our father, but he who possesses *three* other qualities is of the disciples of Balaam the wicked. A good eye, a humble spirit, and a lowly soul are the qualities of the disciple Abraham our father. An evil eye, a haughty spirit and a proud soul are the qualities of a disciple of Balaam the wicked" (*Ethics of the Fathers* 5:23).

9. "*Three* fine gifts were given to the world: wisdom, strength, and wealth" (*Bamidbar Rabbah* 22:7).

10. "There are *three* persons who have a share in the World to Come: he who resides in Palestine, he who raises children to be scholars, and he who honors the Sabbath" (Talmud *Pesachim* 113a).

11. "*Three* men become aged before their time: he who lives on the upper floor, he who endeavors to raise poultry as a livelihood, and he who gives orders but is not obeyed" (*Otzar Midrashim* 66).

12. "*Three* men are beloved by God: he who does not become angry, he who does not become drunken, and he who does not stand upon his dignity" (Talmud *Pesachim* 113).

13. "On the Sabbath afternoon in services we recite *three* verses beginning with the words 'Thy righteousness.' These are in honor of *three* great men who died on

Sabbath afternoon: Moses, Joseph, and David" (*Zohar* I:156a).

14. "*Three* things weaken eyesight: combing hair that is dry, drinking from a drip, and putting on wet shoes" (Talmud *Pesachim* 111b).

15. "A man has *three* friends: his son, his wealth, and his good deeds" (*Pirke de Rabbi Eliezer* 34).

16. "Israel gave *three* fine gifts to God: modesty, compassion, and loving-kindness" (Jerusalem Talmud, *Sanhedrin* 6, 7).

17. "*Three* are called by the Name of God: *tzaddikim* (Righteous Ones), the Messiah, and Jerusalem" (Talmud *Bava Batra* 75b).

18. "*Three* testify, each for the other: God, Israel, and the Torah" (Talmud *Chagigah* 3, *Tosafot*).

19. "There are *three* whom God dislikes: he who speaks one way with his mouth and another in his heart; he who knows of testimony on behalf of a fellow man but does not go forth to present his testimony; he who beholds an immoral act and testifies against it in his role of a single witness" (Talmud *Pesachim* 113b).

20. "*Three* were punished with leprosy because they loved possession and not the Torah: Noah, Cain, and Azariah" (*Otzar Midrashim* 225).

21. "The verse 'And a *threefold* cord is not quickly broken' (Ecclesiastes 4:12) applies to the person who occupies himself with Scripture, with the Oral Law, and with practical ways of the world" (Talmud *Kiddushin* 40).

22. "*Three* things weaken the strength of man: fear, trouble, and sin" (Talmud *Gittin* 70b).

23. "The soul consists of *three* parts: power of life, power of endurance, and the power of higher feeling" (*Zohar* I:81a).

24. "Slander injures *three* persons: the slanderer, the recipient of the slander, and the person slandered" (Talmud *Arakhin* 15b).

25. "*Three* voices gladden the heart: the voice of the Torah, the voice of rain, and the voice of coins" (*Otzar Midrashim* 168, *Midrash Chuppat Eliyahu*).

26. "The Almighty loves *three* kinds of people: one who does not become angry, one who does not become drunk, and one who does not love himself" (Talmud *Pesachim* 113b).

27. "*Three* species of creatures hate each other: dogs, roosters, and sorcerers. *Three* love each other: strangers, slaves, and crows" (Talmud *Pesachim* 113b).

28. "*Three* creatures grow stronger as they grow older: the fish, the serpent, and the pig" (Talmud *Shabbat* 77b).

29. "Food remains undigested in the stomach of the dog for *three* days, because God knows that its food is scanty" (Talmud *Shabbat* 155b).

30. "*Three* maladies are remedied by dates: a troubled mind, constipation, and hemorrhoids. Dates are excellent after the morning and evening meal but harmful in the afternoon. They are best at noon" (Talmud *Ketubot* 10b).

31. "*Three* things are pleasant to their possessor: the pleasure of a place in the eyes of its inhabitants, a woman in the eyes of her husband, and a purchase in the eyes of its buyer" (Talmud *Sotah* 47a).

32. "It takes *three* years for the following to give birth: the wolf, lion, bear, leopard, hyena, elephant, ape, and long-tailed ape" (Talmud *Bekhorot* 8a).

33. "During the first *three* months of pregnancy, the child lies in the lower part of the womb. During the next *three* months, it occupies the middle part; and during the last *three* months it is in the upper part. Before parturition, it turns over and this causes birth pains. Those caused by a female child are more severe than those caused by a male" (Talmud *Niddah* 31a).

34. "There are *three* partners in every child: God, the father, and the mother. The father's share consists of all that is white, which includes the bones, veins, nails, brain, and the white of the eye; the mother's share consists of all that is red—skin, flesh, hair, and the black part of the eye; God's share consists of the breath, the soul, the physiogomy, sight, hearing, speech, motive power, understanding, wisdom. When man departs from this world, God removes His share, leaving only those of the father and mother" (Talmud *Niddah* 31a).

35. "*Three* things are good in a little measure and evil in large measure: yeast, salt, and hesitation" (Talmud *Berakhot* 34).

36. "How many times daily ought a man to pray? So taught our teachers: One should not pray more than *three* times daily, for the *three* patriarchs instituted the *three* statutory prayers: Abraham, the morning service [Genesis 19:27], Isaac, the afternoon service [Genesis 24:63], and Jacob, the evening service [Genesis 28:11]. Daniel, too, prayed *three* times daily on his knees [Daniel 6:10]" (*Tanchuma B., Mikketz* 98a).

37. "The following *three* things are of equal importance: wisdom, fear of God, and humility" (Talmud *Derech Eretz Rabbah* 57a).

38. "The rabbis say: *Three* combine in the making of men: God and father and mother. If men honor their father and mother, God says, 'I reckon it to them as if I dwelt among them, and as if they honored me' " (Talmud *Kiddushin* 30b).

39. "Rabbi Chanina taught: All who go down to hell will come up again except *three:* the adulterer, the one who puts his fellow to shame in public and the one who calls his fellow by an opprobrious name" (Talmud *Bava Metziah,* 58b).

40. There are *three* crowns: the crown of the Torah, the crown of the priesthood, and the crown of the Kingdom. Aaron was worthy of the crown of the priesthood and obtained it, David was worthy of the crown of the Kingdom and obtained it. The crown of the Torah remains overall so that no person shall have the pretext to say, 'If the crown of the priesthood and the crown of the Kingdom were yet available, I would have proved myself worthy of them and have obtained them.' For the crown of the Torah is available for all" (*Sifre Numbers Korach* 119).

41. "Guests ought not to take from what is set before them and give thereof to the host's son or daughter without asking his leave first. Once, in a year of drought, it happened that *three* guests were invited by a man who had but *three* eggs to offer them. When the host's son entered, one guest took his portion and gave it to the child and the other guests did likewise. The host, entering, found his son with one piece in his mouth and two

in his hands. He beat the child to the ground, and the child died. When the mother saw this, she threw herself from the roof, and then the father too threw himself down. Thus, said Rabbi Eliezer ben Jacob, *three* died for this thing'' (Talmud *Chullin* 94a).

42. "Rabbi Elazar said: *Three* times did Moses come into the category of error because he gave way to anger [Leviticus 10:16, Numbers 20:10 and Numbers 31:14]'' (*Sifre Numbers, Mattot* 157).

43. "*Three* gifts were created in the world. If a man has obtained any one of them, he has acquired the desire of all the world: if he has obtained wisdom, he has obtained everything; if he has obtained strength, he has obtained everything; if he has obtained riches, he has obtained everything. But when? When these things are the gifts of God, and come to him through the power of the Torah, but the strength and the riches of flesh and blood are worth nothing at all, and if they come not from God, they will be taken from him at the end'' (*Midrash Numbers Rabbah, Mattot* 22:7).

44. "*Three* kings and four private persons have no share in the World to Come. The *three* kings are Jeroboam, Ahav, and Manasseh'' (Talmud *Sanhedrin* 11:1).

45. "For the merit of *three* things will rain come down: for the merit of the earth, for the merit of loving-kindness, for the merit of sufferings, and all *three* are indicated in the one verse of Job 37:13: 'He causes it to come whether for correction or for His land, or for mercy' '' (Jerusalem Talmud, *Taanit* 3:3).

46. "*Three* types of people, God hates: the person who says one thing with his mouth and thinks otherwise in his heart; one who could give evidence in

another's favor and does not do so; and one who, being alone, sees a bad deed of his neighbor and gives unsupported evidence against him'' (Talmud *Pesachim* 113b).

47. ''Rabbi Amram said, in the name of Rav: From *three* sins a person cannot escape every day: wicked thoughts, calculation on or inattentiveness during prayer, and slander'' (Talmud *Bava Batra* 164b).

48. ''Why is the slanderous tongue called '*shelishi*' ('third')? Because it slays *three:* he who utters the slander, the one who receives it, and the person of whom it is uttered'' (*Midrash Numbers Rabbah, Chukkat* 19:2).

49. ''Rabbah Yochanan ben Zakkai said: On account of *three* sins the householders were delivered over to the Roman Empire: because they practiced usury and exacted payment for bills already paid and because they promised charity in public but did not give it, and because they removed burdens from themselves and laid them, and also the taxes, upon the poor and needy (*Avot de Rabbi Natan* 34a).

50. ''Rabbi Samuel ben Nachmani said in the name of Rabbi Yudan ben Rabbi Chanina: *Three* times it says, 'Return, according to the *three* times that one must repel a person who seeks to become a proselyte' '' (*Midrash Ruth Rabbah* 16).

51. ''Rabbi Yudan said in the name of Rabbi Elazar: *Three* things annul the evil decree: prayer, repentance, and almsgiving, and all are contained in this one verse: 'If my people shall humble themselves and pray and seek my face, and turn from their evil ways, then will I forgive their sins [2 Chronicles 7:14],' for to seek my face is alsmgiving, as it says, 'Through almsgiving shall I

behold your face [Psalm 17:15]' '' (*Pesikta Kahana* 191a).

52. "*Three* things restore tranquility to the mind: music, fair sights, and sweet smells. *Three* things render a person cheerful: a fair home, a fair wife, and fair chattels" (Talmud *Berakhot* 57b).

53. "Rabbi Judah said in the name of Rav: *Three* things shorten a person's days and years: the refusal to read the lesson when invited to do so; to decline the cup of wine that the leader in grace drinks; to give oneself out as a rabbi" (Talmud *Berakhot* 55a).

54. "A person is known in *three* ways: by his behavior as regards money and drink and by the control of his temper, and some say, by his jokes" (Talmud *Eruvin* 65b).

55. "Rabbi Jose ben Judah said: The width of a column of a Torah scroll must not be less than the width of *three* fingers" (*Soferim* 36a).

56. "Rabbi Huna said: The kingdom of Greece excels the wicked kingdom of Rome in *three* matters: in laws, in keeping records, and in oratorical style" (*Midrash Genesis Rabbah* 16:4).

57. "Rabbi Jonathan said: *Three* things were given as a gift to the world: Torah, luminaries, and rain" (*Midrash Genesis Rabbah* 6:5).

58. "How many *tefillos* is one required to utter every day? Our masters taught: One is to utter no more than the *three tefillos,* which the Fathers of the world ordained. David came and specified the times: 'Evening, morn, and noon [Psalm 55:18].' Hence, one is not permitted to utter more than *three tefillos* a day" (*Tanchuma, Mikketz* 9).

59. "*Three* love one another: proselytes, slaves, and ravens" (Talmud *Pesachim* 113b).

60. "There are *three* wrongs before which the curtain of heaven is never closed: cheating, robbery, and idolatry" (Talmud *Bava Metziah* 59a).

61. "*Three* will not see Gehenna's face: they who undergo the torments of poverty, they who are sick in their bowels, and they who are hounded by the authorities" (Talmud *Eruvin* 41b).

62. "*Three* come unawares: the Messiah, something found, and a scorpion" (Talmud *Sanhedrin* 97a).

63. "The road does *three* things: it wears out one's clothing, grinds down one's body, and diminishes one's money" (Midrash *Tehillim,* ed. S. Buber).

64. "*Three* organs are under man's control: the mouth, the hands, and the feet. *Three* are not under his control: the eyes, the ears, and the nose" (*Tanchuma, Toldot* 12).

65. "The prolonging of *three* acts prolongs a man's days and years: prolonging the *tefillah,* prolonging his stay at the table, and prolonging his stay in the privy" (Talmud *Berakhot* 54b).

66. "*Three* things nullify an evil decree: prayer, charity, and repentance" (Jerusalem Talmud, *Taanit* 5:1).

67. "*Three* things deplete a person's strength: fear, travel, and sin" (Talmud *Gittin* 70a).

68. "*Three* things take away a person's reason and belief in one's Creator: idolatry, an evil spirit, and the torments of poverty" (Talmud *Eruvin* 41b).

69. "*Three* things are said about finger and toenails: He who burns them is a pious man, he who buries them

is a righteous man, and he who throws them away is a wicked man" (Talmud *Niddah* 7a).

70. "*Three* things were given conditionally: the Land of Israel, the Temple, and the royal house of David" (*Mechilta de Rabbi Ishmael, Yitro*).

71. "There are *three* things whose sound goes from one end of the world to the other, and though mortals are in between, they are not aware of it: the sound of the day's sun revolving on its course, the sound of rain clouds moving across the firmament, and the sound of the soul when it leaves the body" (*Midrash Genesis Rabbah* 6:7).

72. "*Three* things God intended to create, and if God had not willed them, it would be but right that He should think of them. And these are: Concerning a corpse, that it should become offensive; and concerning a dead person, that he should be forgotten from one's mind; and concerning produce, that it should rot . . ." (Talmud *Pesachim* 54b).

73. "*Three* things are grave threats to the body: heart disease, disease of the bowels, and an empty purse—which is a graver threat to the body than the preceding two" (*Midrash Ecclesiastes Rabbah* 7:26).

74. "There are *three* things of which a large quantity and a small quantity are bad, while a moderate quantity is good: leaven, salt, and a refusal of an invitation. At first one should decline, then one should hesitate, but finally one should eagerly accept" (Jerusalem Talmud, *Berakhot* 5:3).

75. "*Three* things are equal in importance: the earth, rain, and man. And in the Hebrew each of these words is made up of *three* letters. This teaches that if

there were no earth, there would be no rain; if there were no rain, the earth would not endure; and if there were neither, man could not exist" (*Midrash Genesis Rabbah* 13:3).

76. "For *three* the Holy One cries every day: for him who could occupy himself with Torah but does not; for him who cannot occupy himself with Torah yet does; and for a leader who lords it over the community" (Talmud *Chagigah* 5b).

77. "*Three* have returned to the place where they first came into being: Israel, Egypt's money, and the script of the Tablets" (Talmud *Pesachim* 87b).

78. "There are *three* whose life is no life: he who has to rely on his neighbor's table, he whose wife rules him, and he whose body is racked by suffering" (Talmud *Betzah* 32b).

79. "There are *three* whose life is not life: those who are too compassionate, those who are too prone to anger, and those who are too fastidious" (Talmud *Pesachim* 113b).

80. "Suffering is divided into *three* portions: the patriarchs and all the generations of men took one, the generation that lived in the time of Hadrian's persecution took one, and the lord Messiah will take one" (*Midrash Tehillim*, ed. S. Buber).

81. "There are *three* whose sins are forgiven: the proselyte, the one who rises to an important office, and the one who weds a wife" (Jerusalem Talmud, *Bikkurim* 3:3).

82. "There are *three* concerning whom the Holy One makes proclamation every day: the bachelor who lives in a large city but does not succumb to sin, the

poor man who returns a lost article to its rightful
owner, and the rich man who tithes his produce in
privacy'' (Talmud *Pesachim* 113a).

83. ''There are *three* who will inherit the World to
Come: he who lives in the Land of Israel, he who brings
up his sons to the study of Torah, and he who recites the
Havdalah blessing over wine as a farewell to the Sabbath'' (Talmud *Pesachim* 113a).

84. ''*Three* bear witness in behalf of one another:
the Holy One, Israel, and the Sabbath'' (Tosafot on
Chagigah 3b).

85. ''In the hand of the Holy One, there are *three*
keys that no creature, neither an angel nor a seraph, can
take possession of: the key to rain, the key to the womb,
and the key to the grave at the resurrection of the dead''
(Talmud *Taanit* 2a).

86. ''*Three* take in abundance and give in abundance: the earth, the sea, and the Roman government''
(*Midrash Leviticus Rabbah* 4:2).

87. ''There are *three* insolent ones: Israel among the
nations, a dog among beasts, and the cock among fowls
(Talmud *Betzah* 25b).

88. ''*Three* cry and receive no response from a court
on earth or in heaven: he who has money and lends it
without witnesses, he who acquires a master for himself, and he whose wife rules him'' (Talmud *Bava
Metziah* 75b).

89. ''There are *three* things for which one entreats
God's mercy: a good king, a good year, and a good
dream'' (Talmud *Berakhot* 55a).

90. ''*Three* sounds go from one end of the world to
the other: the sound of the sun's orb, the sound of

Rome's tumult, and the sound of the soul when it leaves the body" (Talmud *Yoma* 20b).

91. "*Three* things are hard to take in excess, but just right in limited measure: leaven, salt, and declining an invitation" (Talmud *Berakhot* 34a).

92. "*Three* men made requests in careless language: two received favorable answers and one an unfavorable answer. The *three:* Abraham's servant Eliezer, Saul son of Kish, and Jephthah the Gileadite. As to Abraham's servant Eliezer, he requested, 'So let it come to pass, that the damsel to whom I shall say: Let down your pitcher, I pray you, that I may drink. . . . You have appointed for Your servant, even for Isaac [Genesis 24:14],' a request that could have included a lame or a blind damsel. However, he was answered favorably in that Rebekah came out to meet him. As to Saul, son of Kish, it was requested in his behalf, 'And it shall be, that the man who kills Goliath, the king will enrich him with great riches, and will give him his daughter, and make his father's house free in Israel [1 Samuel 17:25],' a request that might have included a slave or a bastard. However, he was answered favorably in that David came forth. As to Jephthah the Gileadite, he requested, 'Then it shall be, that whatsoever comes forth of the doors of my house to meet me when I return in peace from the children of Ammon, it shall be for God, and I will offer it up for a burnt offering [Judges 11:31],' a request that might have included an unclean creature unfit for an offering. And, indeed, he was answered unfavorably in that his own daughter came out of his house" (Talmud *Taanit* 4a).

93. "A person is called by *three* names: one given to him by his father and mother, one that others call him, and one that through his deeds he causes himself to be called" (*Midrash, Ecclesiastes Rabbah* 7:1).

94. "One man differs from his fellow in *three* ways: in voice, in appearance, and in understanding" (Talmud *Sanhedrin* 38a).

95. "In *three* instances a man is apt to die because Satan is ready to bring charges against him: when he lives in a house on the verge of collapsing, when he walks on a road by himself, or when he sets out on the Great Mediterranean Sea" (*Midrash, Ecclesiastes Rabbah* 3:2).

96. For *three* reasons one should not enter a dilapidated house: because of suspicion of lewdness, because of its possible collapse, and because of demons" (Talmud *Berakhot* 3a).

97. "*Three* good gifts—Torah, the Land of Israel, and the World to Come—the Holy One bestowed on Israel, and they were bestowed only through suffering" (Talmud *Berakhot* 5a).

98. "There are *three* kinds of torpor: the torpor of sleep, the torpor of prophecy, and the torpor of unconsciousness" (Talmud *Genesis Rabbah* 17:6).

99. "To *three* things the Torah is likened: to the desert, to fire, and to water. This is to tell you that just as these *three* things are free to all who come into the world, so also are the worlds of the Torah free to all who come into the world" (*Mechilta de Rabbi Ishmael,* Exodus 20:2).

Three as Completeness

The number three is also latent in a number of rabbinic passages where it expresses completeness. Here are several examples of triads of phrases in rabbinic teaching.

1. "Jose ben Joezer of Zeredah said: Let your house be a meeting place for the sages, and sit amid the dust of their feet, and drink in their words with thirst" (*Ethics of the Fathers* 1:4).

2. "Jose ben Jochanan of Jerusalem said: Let your house be open wide, and let the needy be members of your household, and talk not much with women!" (*Ethics of the Fathers* 1:5).

3. "Joshua ben Perachya said: Provide yourself with a teacher and get yourself a student companion and judge all men favorably" (*Ethics of the Fathers* 1:6).

4. "Shemayah said: Love work, hate mastery, and seek no intimacy with the ruling power" (*Ethics of the Fathers* 1:10).

5. "Shammai said: Make Torah study a fixed habit, say little and do much, and receive all men with a cheerful countenance" (*Ethics of the Fathers* 1:15).

6. "Rabban Gamliel said: Provide yourself with a teacher and remove from yourself doubt, and tithe not too much by guesswork" (*Ethics of the Fathers* 1:16).

7. "Rabbi Joshua said: The evil eye, the evil impulse, and hatred of mankind put a man out of this world" (*Ethics of the Fathers* 2:16).

8. "Rabbi Ishmael said: Be submissive to a superior, and kindly to the young, and receive all men cheerfully" (*Ethics of the Fathers* 3:16).

9. "Rabbi Elezzar ha-Kappar said: Jealousy, lust, and ambition put a man out of this world" (*Ethics of the Fathers* 4:28).

10. "Three things drain a person's health: worry, travel, and sin" (Talmud *Gittin* 70a).

11. "*Three* types of persons are termed epicurean heretics: he who says that there is no prophecy at all and that there is no knowledge that emanates from the Creator and reaches the hearts of men; he who denies the prophecy of Moses; he who says that the Creator is not aware of human actions. Each of these three is an epicurean heretic" (*Mishneh Torah,* "Laws of Repentance," no. 8).

THE NUMBER THREE IN JEWISH LIFE

The following is a list of threes as they appear in various aspects of Jewish life.

1. Three patriarchs: Abraham, Isaac, and Jacob.
2. Three angels visit Abraham, who, according to rabbinic tradition, are said to be Raphael, Gavriel, and Michael.
3. Three sounds of the shofar (ram's horn): *tekiah, shevarim,* and *teruah.*
4. Three matzos used at the Passover seder.
5. Three sections of the Jewish Bible (Tanakh): Torah, Nevi'im (Prophets), and Ketuvim (Writings).
6. Three rabbinic commandments specifically for women to perform: Taking challah, going to the *mikveh,* and lighting Sabbath candles.
7. Three meals during the Sabbath.

8. Three themes discussed in the Passover Haggadah: Pesach, matzo, and *maror.*

9. Three *hadasim* (myrtle) leaves used in the *lulav* (palm) holder.

10. Minimum of three persons required to say aloud the Grace after the Meal.

11. Three people called to the Torah on a regular weekday Monday or Thursday morning.

12. Three different categories of Jews: Kohen (priestly tribe), Levi (levitical tribe), and Yisrael (Israelite).

13. Three years of age is the time when a traditional Jew gives his son his first haircut.

14. Three judges required for a *Bet Din* (Court of Jewish Law).

15. Triennial reading (i.e., every three years) of the Torah.

THE NUMBER FOUR

THE NUMBER FOUR IN THE BIBLE

It has been said that the number four is probably derived from the four cardinal points of the compass (some point to the square). For the Hebrews, four was an important number. One explanation for its significance is that the Name of God, "YHVH," is spelled in Hebrew with four letters. In various parts of the world, the number four is sacred and signifies completeness or perfection. Here is a collection of places in the Bible where the number four plays a prominent role.

1. In Genesis 2:10: "a river issues from Eden to water the garden, and it then divides and becomes *four* branches. The name of the first is Pishon[,] . . . the name of the second is Gichon[,] . . . the name of the third Tigris and the *fourth* river is the Euphrates."

2. In Ezekiel 14:21 there are four horrific punishments: "How much less should any escape now that I have let loose against Jerusalem all *four* of my terrible punishments—the sword, famine, wild beasts, and pestilence."

3. In Zechariah 2:1 there are four horns that scatter Judah: "I looked up, and I saw *four* horns. I asked the angel who talked with me, 'What are those?' 'Those,' he replied, 'are the horns that tossed Judah, Israel, and Jerusalem.' "

4. In Exodus 25 and following, the number four appears in the measurements of the furniture of the Tabernacle: "Cast *four* rings for it, to be attached to its *four* feet."

5. The bearers of God's throne in the Prophet Ezekiel's famous theophany are four: "Each of them had a human face; each of the *four* had the face of a lion on the right; each of the *four* had the face of an ox on the left; and each of the *four* had the face of an eagle on the back" (Ezekiel 1:10).

6. The Hebrews believed that the earth had four "quarters" from which four winds emanated: "And I shall bring *four* winds against Elam from the *four* quarters of heaven, and scatter them to all those winds" (Jeremiah 49:36).

7. Multiples of four are discernible in the length of the Tabernacle curtains—28 cubits (Exodus 26:2). In addition, forty years was considered the length of a generation, and forty was the number of years that the Israelites wandered after the Exodus, and the number of days that Moses spent atop Mount Sinai.

THE NUMBER FOUR IN RABBINIC THOUGHT

The number four appears with a fair amount of frequency in rabbinic writings. Here is a sampling of some of those teachings.

1. "*Four* things cause a man to age prematurely: a fright, anger, children, and an evil-natured wife" (*Tanchuma Chaye Sarah*).

2. "*Four* Rabbis indulged in theosophy: Rabbi Akiba, Rabbi Elisha ben Abuyah, Simeon ben Azzai, and Simeon ben Zoma. Ben Azzai looked and died; Ben Zoma looked and lost his mind; Elisha Acher cut down the plants of the Torah. Only Rabbi Akiba made his exit in safety" (Talmud *Chagigah* 14b).

3. "*Four* things receive a penalty in this world, but the principal remains in the World to Come: idolatry, incest, bloodshed, and an evil tongue. The last is most pernicious" (Jerusalem Talmud, *Peah* 1:1).

4. "*Four* classes of men will never see God's face— the scoffer, the liar, the slanderer, and the hypocrite" (Talmud *Sotah* 42a).

5. "When men learned subjects of Torah, *four* various countenances may be observed: if the student has a somber aspect, he is learning the Scriptures; if his countenance is neither serious nor frivolous, he is learning the Mishnah; if he seems to be interested, he is reasoning in *halachah* [Jewish law]; and if his face be merry, he is occupied with *Aggadah* [legend]" (*Pesikta Rabbati* 21:6).

6. "Rabbi Judah in the name of Rav said: *Four* should offer thanksgiving prayers: Those who have landed safely after a sea voyage; those who have returned from desert travel; those who have recovered from a serious illness; and those who have been liberated from prison" (Talmud *Berakhot* 54b).

7. "When a divorced man marries a divorced woman, there are *four* minds in bed" (Talmud *Pesachim* 112a).

8. "At *four* periods pestilence increases: in the fourth year, in the seventh, at the conclusion of the seventh year, and at the conclusion of the Feast of Tabernacles in every year" (*Ethics of the Fathers* 5:13).

9. "There are *four* types of character: Easy to provoke and easy to appease—his loss is cancelled by his gain; hard to provoke and hard to appease—his gain is cancelled by his loss; hard to provoke and easy to appease—he is a saintly man; easy to provoke and hard to appease—he is a wicked man" (*Ethics of the Fathers* 5:15).

10. "There have been *four* women in the world's history who could truly be termed 'beautiful,' aside from Eve, who was not born but created. They are Sarah, Abigail, Rachab, and Esther" (Talmud *Megillah* 15a).

11. "One cup of wine is good for a woman, two make her disgraceful, three demoralizing, and *four* are brutalizing" (Talmud *Ketubot* 65a).

12. "*Four* kinds of persons are considered as if dead: the pauper, the leper, the blind person, and the childless one" (Talmud *Nedarim* 64a).

13. "*Four* individuals were named before their birth: Isaac, Ishmael, Josiah, and Solomon" (Jerusalem Talmud, *Berakhot* 1:6).

14. "*Four* languages are ideal for *four* purposes: Greek for poetry, Latin for war, Aramaic for lamentation, and Hebrew for speech" (Jerusalem Talmud, *Sotah* 7:2).

15. "On account of *four* things is the sun in eclipse; on account of an *Av Bet Din* who died and was not fittingly mourned; on account of a betrothed maiden who cried out aloud in the city and there was none to

rescue her; on account of sodomy; and on account of two brothers whose blood was shed at the same time" (Talmud *Derech Eretz Rabbah* 56a).

16. "On account of *four* things are the luminaries in eclipse: on account of those who forge documents, on account of those who give false evidence, on account of those who breed small cattle, and on account of those who cut down good trees" (Talmud *Derech Eretz Rabbah* 56a).

17. "On account of *four* things the wealth of householders is confiscated by the government: on account of those who retain in their possession bills which have been paid; on account of those who lend money on usury; on account of those who had the power to protest [against wrongdoing] and failed to do so; and on account of those who publicly donate specified sums for charity and do not give them" (Talmud *Derech Eretz Rabbah* 56a).

18. "*Four perutot* are without a sign of blessing: They are the wages of scribes, the wages of interpreters, money that came from overseas, and he who marries for the sake of a dowry. These will not be able to bequeath anything to their children or grandchildren" (Talmud *Derech Eretz Zutah* 58b–59a).

19. "Rabbi Jose ben Chanina said that Moses made *four* declarations and then *four* prophets came after him and annulled them. Of these *four,* the fourth was Ezekiel, for whereas Moses said, 'He visited the sins of the fathers upon the child [Exodus 20:5],' Ezekiel came and annulled the assertion, even as it says, 'The soul that sins, that soul shall die [Ezekiel 18:20]' " (Talmud *Makkot* 24a).

20. " 'Whoso loves correction loves knowledge [Proverbs 12:1].' *Four* were beaten. One kicked, one laughed, one besought his friend, and one said, 'Why hangs the strap? Beat me with it.' One kicked, that is Job, as it is said, 'I say to God, do not condemn me. Make me know wherefore you contend with me [Job 10:2].' 'Why am I beaten? What have I done to you? Wherein have I sinned? Make known to me my transgression [Job 13:23].' 'I know that you have the power, and that you can deal thus with me. O earth, cover unto you my blood [Job 16:18].' Thus Job kicked. The second was beaten and laughed. That is Abraham, as it is said, 'And Abraham fell upon his face and laughed [Genesis 17:17].' The case of Abraham is like the case of a man who beat his son because he had sworn to beat him, and he said to his son, 'I have sworn to beat you.' The son said, 'The power is yours.' So he beat him, thinking that his son would say, 'Enough.' When the father had beaten him, he said, 'I have beaten him enough.' So God said to Abraham, 'I am God Almighty. I am He who says to My world, It is enough. I am He who says about your testing, It is enough.' The third besought his friend. That is Hezekiah, as it says, 'He prayed to God [Isaiah 38:2], turning his face to the wall.' The fourth said, 'Why hangs the strap? Beat me with it.' That is David, who said, 'Judge me, O God [Psalm 26:1]' " (*Midrash Psalms* on 26:1, I, 108a, par. 2).

21. "Rabbi Simeon used to say: For *four* reasons a man who leaves the corner of his field for the poor [Leviticus 19:9] should choose the end of his field. First, so as not to rob the poor. For a man might seize a suitable opportunity and tell a poor relative to take the

produce from the near corner. Second, so that the poor
may not have to wait all day but may be able to go and
gather elsewhere, and come back to him when the end
of his field is being cut. Third, for appearance sake, so
that the passersby should not say: 'See how so-and-so
has reaped his field and has not left a corner for the
poor.' And fourth, because the Law says: 'You shall not
reap the end corner of your field' '' (*Sifra* 87c).

22. "For *four* reasons a man should rebuke others
only just before he dies: so as not to have to reprove him
again and again. So that he should not feel shame in the
presence of the reprover, whenever he should happen
to see him. So that he should feel nothing in his heart
against the reprover, and so that the reprover should
part from him in peace, for reproof then brings him to
peace" (*Sifre Deuteronomy, Devarim,* par. 2).

23. "For *four* sins is rain held back: idolatry, un-
chastity, bloodshed, and because of those who promise
publicly to give charity and do not give it" (Jerusalem
Talmud, *Taanit* 3:3).

24. "*Four* things are unseemly for a scholar: to walk
out at night, to smell of scent in the street, to be among
the last to enter the synagogue, to dally much with the
common folk" (Talmud *Derech Eretz Zutah* 5:2).

25. "Ben Azzai said: Whoever sets the following
four things before his eyes and upon his heart will
never commit a sin: Whence he came, whither he goes,
who is his Judge, and what he is destined to become"
(*Derech Eretz Rabbah* 3:1).

26. "Rabbi Joshua ben Levi said: Israel's redemption
is compared to *four* things: to harvesting, to vintaging,
to gathering of spices, and to a woman with child.

"It is compared to harvesting, because when a field is harvested prematurely, even the straw is unusable; if the field is harvested in its proper time, even the straw is fully usable. Hence Scripture: 'Put in the sickle, for the harvest is ripe [Joel 4:13].'

"It is compared to vintaging, because when a vineyard is vintaged before its time, even the vinegar made from it is not good; but if gathered in its time, even its vinegar is good. Thus: 'Sing you of her: a vineyard of foaming wine [Isaiah 27:2]'—only when the grapes in the vineyard are full of juice are you to gather them.

"It is compared to spices, because if spices are gathered when they are still moist and soft, they do not give off fragrance. But if gathered when they are dry, they give off fragrance, as is said, 'That the spices thereof may flow out [Song of Songs 4:16].'

"It is compared to a woman with child, because if the woman gives birth before the time, the child will not live; but if at the right time, the child lives. So it is written, 'Therefore God will give them up until the time that she who travails has brought forth [Micah 5:2]' " (*Midrash Song of Songs Rabbah* 8:14).

27. "There are *four* things commonly used in the world, for each of which, when lost, a substitute is available: 'There is a mine for silver, and a place for gold which they refine. Iron is taken out of the dust, and brass is molten out of the stone [Job 28:1–2].' Each of these metals, when lost, has a substitute" (Jerusalem Talmud, *Berakhot* 2:8).

28. "*Four* companies of ministering angels utter praise before the Holy One, blessed be He: the first camp, that of Michael, at God's right; the second camp,

that of Gabriel, at God's left; the third camp, that of Uriel, in front of God; and the fourth camp, that of Raphael, behind God'' (*Pirke de Rabbi Eliezer* 4).

29. ''*Four* are hard to put up with: a poor man who is proud, a rich man who falsely denies a claim against him, an old man who is lecherous, and a leader who without justification lords it over his community'' (Talmud *Pesachim* 113b).

30. ''The Holy One showed Abraham *four* things— Gehenna, the yoke of the heathen kingdoms, the giving of Torah, and the Temple—and said to him: If your children are deeply occupied with the latter two, they will be saved from the former two'' (*Midrash Genesis Rabbah* 44:21).

31. ''*Four* things tear up a Divine decree issued against a person: charity, supplication, a change of name and a change of conduct'' (Talmud *Rosh Hashanah* 16b).

32. ''*Four* things drain a person's strength: iniquity, wayfaring, fasting, and the Roman Empire'' (*Midrash Lamentations Rabbah* 1:14).

33. ''*Four* are called scoundrel: the person who raises his hand against a neighbor to strike him, even though he does not strike him; one who borrows and does not repay; one who is brazen-faced, and one who quarrels'' (*Tanchuma, Korach* 8).

34. ''There are *four* that the Holy One regrets having created: exile, Chaldeans, Ishmaelites, and the impulse to evil'' (Talmud *Sukkah* 52b).

35. ''*Four* things need to be done with vigor: Torah study, good deeds, prayer, and one's daily task'' (Talmud *Berakhot* 32b).

36. "How do we know that *four* cups of wine are required [on Passover]? Rabbi Yochanan said in the name of Rabbi Benayah that they correspond to the *four* redemptions. Rabbi Levi said that they correspond to the *four* empires, and the Rabbis said that they correspond to the *four* cups of wrath that God shall one day give the heathen to drink" (Jerusalem Talmud, *Pesachim* 37b).

37. "For *four* reasons the children of Israel were not redeemed from Egypt: they did not change their names, they did not change their language, they did not reveal their secrets, and they were not wanton" (*Midrash Psalms* 114:4).

38. "*Four* kinds of shade are haunted by demons: the shade of a single date palm, the shade of a kinnara, the shade of a caper, and the shade of thorny bushes whose fronds are made edible" (Talmud *Pesachim* 111b).

THE NUMBER FOUR IN JEWISH LIFE

The number four appears with much frequency throughout Jewish life. Here is a list of several examples.

1. Four matriarchs: Sarah, Rebekkah, Rachel, and Leah.
2. Four garments worn by a *Kohen*.
3. Four cups of wine drunk at the seder.
4. Four questions asked at the seder.
5. Four sons in the Passover Haggadah.
6. Four species used on the Festival of Sukkot—*lulav, etrog,* myrtle, and palm branches.
7. Four corners on a *tallit* (prayer shawl).
8. Four pieces of parchment in the head box of a pair of phylacteries.

9. Four different terms used in the Bible to express the Israelite redemption from Egypt.

10. Four rows of precious stones on the breastplate worn by the High Priest.

11. Four sections of the Code of Jewish Law: *Orach Chayyim, Yoreh De'ah, Even Ha'Ezer,* and *Choshen Mishpat.*

THE NUMBER FIVE

THE NUMBER FIVE IN THE BIBLE

The meaning of the number five is unknown. It seems to have been important, especially in sacred literature, where it occurs as a frequent division—such as the Five Books of Moses or the five chapters of the Book of Lamentations. It is a basic number that dates back to remote antiquity. There was a primitive Hamatic system based on the number five before the decimal system. The number five seems quite obviously derived from the fingers of the hand used by early man in his simple arithmetic calculations. It is also, in the Bible, related to both the decimal and sexagesimal systems.

Occasionally, the number five seems to be a bad number—five was the number of Midianite kings that Gideon fought and five was also the number of Philistine princes who ordered Samson caught.

Here is sampling of biblical references to the number five.

1. In the Books of 2 Kings 7:13, it appears the number five is used to mean simply "a few": "But one of the courtiers spoke up, 'Let *five* of the remaining horses that

are still here be taken—they are like those that are left here of the whole multitude of Israel, out of the whole multitude of Israel that have perished—and let us send and find out.' ''

2. In Genesis 43:34, the number five also appears to mean "a few": "Portions were served them from his table; but Benjamin's portion was *five* times that of anyone else."

3. Like the number four, the number five also appears in connection with sacred architecture (1 Kings 7:39, 49): "He disposed the laver stands, *five* at the right side of the house and *five* at its left side. . . . And the lamp stands—*five* on the right side and *five* on the left."

4. The number five is also occasionally found in connection with penalties (Exodus 21:37): "When a man steals an ox or a sheep, and slaughters it or sells it, he shall pay *five* oxen for the ox."

5. The number five also appears in the Bible in connection with the theme of redemption (Numbers 3:47 and 18:16): "And as the redemption price of the 273 Israelite firstborn over and above the number of Levites, take *five* shekels per head. . . . Take as their redemption price from the age of one month up, the money equivalent of *five* shekels by the sanctuary weight."

6. The number five also appears with frequency in connection with gifts (Genesis 43:34 and 45:22): "Portions were served them from his table, but Benjamin's portion was *five* times that of anyone else. To each of them, moreover, he gave a change of clothing; but to Benjamin he gave three hundred pieces of silver and *five* changes of clothing."

7. The number five is often used as a small round number: "*Five* of you shall give chase to one hundred" (Leviticus 26:8). "In that day, there shall be *five* towns in the land of Egypt speaking the language of Canaan and swearing loyalty to the Lord of Hosts" (Isaiah 19:18).

8. The fraction one-fifth is also quite common in the Bible (Leviticus 5:16 and 22:14): "He shall make restitution for that wherein he was remiss about the sacred things, and he shall add a *fifth* part to it and give it to the priest. . . . But if a man eats of a sacred donation unwittingly, he shall pay the priest for the sacred donation, adding *one-fifth* of its value."

9. Other multiples of the number five appear elsewhere in the Bible, including the multiples of 50 all the way up to the multiple of 500,000. These will be presented later on in the book.

THE NUMBER FIVE IN RABBINIC THOUGHT

1. "*Five* things characterize the Beadle: he is unusually tall, impudent, strong of arm, abundant of strength, and lacking manners" (*Otzar Midrashim* 147).

2. "We find that *five* things may cancel the harsh decree of heaven against a person: almsgiving, prayer, change of name, reformation of conduct, and change of residence.

"Of charity it is written [Proverbs 10:2], 'But almsgiving saves from death.'

"Of prayer it is written: 'Then they cried to God in their trouble, and God delivered them out of their distresses [Psalm 107:6].'

"Of change of name we know that after Sarai changed her name to Sarah, her state of barrenness was changed.

"Of reformation of conduct, we read in Jonah 3:10: 'And God saw their works, that they turned from their evil way, and God repented of the evil, which He said He would do to them; and God did it not.'

"Of change of residence, it is written, 'And God said to Abraham, "Get you out' " [Genesis 12:1], and then it is said: 'I will make of you a great nation' " (Genesis 12:2).

3. "*Five* have no easy forgiveness of sins: he who sins in many ways; he who repents many times of the same sin; he who sins in a sinless age; he who sins in order to repent; he who causes the Holy Name to be profaned" (*Avot de Rabbi Nathan,* ch. 39).

4. "The words 'Bless the Lord, O my soul [Psalm 103:104]' were said *five* times by David with reference to both God and the soul. As God fills the whole world, so does the soul fill the whole body; as God sees and is not seen, so with the soul; as God nourishes the whole world, so does the soul nourish the whole body; as God is pure, so also is the soul pure; as God dwells in secret, so does the soul. Therefore, let him who possesses these *five* properties praise God to whom these *five* attributes belong" (Talmud *Berakhot* 10a).

5. "Rabbi Akiba said: 'He who marries a woman not suited to him violates *five* precepts: (1) Thou shall not avenge; (2) Thou shall not bear a grudge; (3) Thou shall not hate thy brother in thy heart; (4) Thou shall love thy neighbor as thyself; (5) And that thy brother may live with thee. For if he hates her, he wishes she were dead" (*Avot de Rabbi Nathan,* ch. 26).

6. "*Five* things were said of garlic: It satisfies your hunger, keeps your body warm, makes your face bright, increases a man's potency, and kills parasites in the bowels. Some people say that it also encourages love and removes jealousy" (Talmud *Berakhot* 82a).

7. "*Five* things contain a sixtieth part of *five* other things: fire is a sixtieth of hell; honey a sixtieth of manna; the Sabbath a sixtieth of the rest in the World to Come; sleep a sixtieth of death; and a dream, a sixtieth of prophecy" (Talmud *Berakhot* 57b).

8. "*Five* things should be killed even on the Sabbath: the Egyptian fly, Nineveh hornet, Adiabenean scorpion, the serpent, and the mad dog" (Talmud *Shabbat* 121b).

9. "A mad dog is recognized by *five* symptoms: its mouth gapes wide, its lavers, its ears hang down, its tail is curled between its legs, and it slinks along the side of the road. And some add that it barks, but its voice is not heard" (Talmud *Yoma* 83b).

10. "The sacred fire upon the altar had five unusual characteristics: it crouched there like a lion; it shone like the sun; its flames had substance; it consumed liquids as though they were dry materials; it emitted no smoke" (Talmud *Yoma* 21b).

11. "There are *five* sorts of terror that the strong have of the weak: the fear of the lion of the gnat, the elephant of the mosquito, the scorpion of the spider, the eagle of the swallow, and the leviathan of the stickleback" (Talmud *Shabbat* 77b).

12. "*Five* possessions did the Holy One take to Himself in His world, and these are: The Torah, heaven and earth, Abraham, Israel, and the Temple" (*Ethics of the Fathers* 6:10).

13. "King David dwelled in *five* worlds and composed a song for each of them. When he abode in his mother's womb he uttered the song 'Bless God, O my soul, and all within which I am, bless God's Holy Name [Psalm 103:1].' When he came out into the air of the world and beheld the stars and planets, he uttered a song, 'Bless God, you His angels. . . . Bless God, all you His hosts [Psalm 103:20–21].' When, as he sucked milk from his mother's breast and beheld her nipples, he uttered a song, 'Bless God, O my soul, and forget not all those weaned from their mother's milk [Psalm 103:2].' When he saw the downfall of the wicked, he uttered a song, 'The sinners are consumed out of the earth, and the wicked are no more. Bless, God, O my soul, Halleluyah [Psalm 104:35].' When he reflected on the day of death, he uttered a song, 'Bless God, O my soul, You are very great. You are clothed with glory and majesty [Psalm 104:1].' (Talmud *Berakhot* 10a)."

14. " 'And it came to pass when the Benjamite made mention of the Ark of God, Eli fell backward . . . and his neck broke [1 Samuel 4:18].' Rabbi Joshua bar Nechemia said: Neither *five* iron claws nor *five* iron styles killed Eli, but at the news that the Ark was captured, his neck broke" (*Midrash Samuel* 11).

15. " 'And the priest that is greatest among his brothers [Leviticus 21:10].' Why was he called the 'greatest'? Because he was the greatest in *five* matters—in comeliness, in strength, in wealth, in wisdom, and in personality" (Jerusalem Talmud, *Yoma* 1:2).

16. "Rabbi Isaac said: Why is the meal offering distinguished in that *five* kinds of oil dishes are listed in connection with it? A parable provides the answer: A

king of flesh and blood had a friend who was soon to prepare a feast for him. Since the king knew that his friend was poor, he said: Prepare for me whatever you have as *five* kinds of flour dishes, so that I may enjoy your company longer" (Talmud *Menachot* 194b).

17. "Rabbi Eleazar said: By *five* things was Israel redeemed from Egypt, and by these very things will they be redeemed in the future: by suffering, by repentance, by the merit of the fathers, by God's compassion, and by the conclusion of the time decreed for their subjection" (*Midrash Deuteronomy Rabbah* 2:14).

18. "Now Moses . . . came to Horeb, the mountain of God [Exodus 3:1]. The mountain had *five* names: the mountain of God, the mountain of Bashan, the mountain of peaks, the mountain of Horeb, and the mountain of Sinai. The mountain of God, because there Israel accepted the godhead of the Holy One, blessed be He. The mountain of Bashan, because everything that man eats with his teeth (*beshen*) is given for the sake of Torah, which was given on the mount. The mountain of peaks (*gavnunim*) pure as cheese (*gevinah*), and pure from every blemish. The mountain of Horeb because from it the Sanhedrin derived power to slay with the sword (*cherev*). Rabbi Samuel ben Nachman says, The idol worshippers receive their sentence from there, as it is said, 'Those nations shall be utterly wasted—*charov yecheravu* [Isaiah 60:12],' from Horeb they shall be destroyed (*yecheravu*). Sinai, because hatred (*sinah*) descended to idolaters thence [as they hated Israel for accepting the Torah]" (*Exodus Rabbah* 2:4).

19. "*Five* things make a person forget his learning: eating something of which a mouse or a cat has eaten,

eating the heart of a beast, frequent consumption of olives, drinking waste bathwater, and washing one's feet one foot above the other" (Talmud *Horayot* 13b).

20. "*Five* things improve one's learning: eating wheat bread, eating a roasted egg without salt, frequent consumption of olive oil, frequent indulgence in wine and spices, and drinking the water that is left from kneading dough" (Talmud *Horayot* 13b).

THE NUMBER FIVE IN JEWISH LIFE

Here is a sample of the variety of places in which the number five appears in Jewish life:

1. The Five Books of Moses—Genesis, Exodus, Leviticus, Numbers, and Deuteronomy.
2. The Five Megillot—Esther, Song of Songs, Lamentations, Ecclesiastes, and Ruth.
3. Five days of the intermediate days of Sukkot in the Diaspora.
4. Five double knots on the fringe of a prayer shawl.
5. Five twigs of willows that are used on the Festival of Hoshanna Rabbah.
6. Five Hebrew letters that have a final letter—*Chof, Mem, Nun, Peh,* and *Tzaddi.*
7. Five sons of Mattathias: Judah, Simeon, Yochanan, Yonatan, and Eliezer.
8. Five renowned disciples of Rabbi Yochanan ben Zakkai: Eliezer ben Hyrcanus, Joshua ben Chananiah, Jose ha-Kohen, Simeon ben Nethanel, and Eleazar ben Arach.
9. Five species of grain: wheat, barley, spelt, oats, and rye.

THE NUMBER SIX

THE NUMBER SIX IN THE BIBLE

The number six is part of the sexagesimal system, but it has relatively little symbolic meaning in the Bible. The number six seems to have been a favored number, being half of a so-called good number, twelve. The following are examples of the occurrence of the number six in the Bible.

1. "*Six* days you shall labor and do all manner of work" (Exodus 20:9).

2. In Exodus 21:2, we learn that six is the maximum number of years of slavery for a slave: "When you acquire a Hebrew slave, he shall serve *six* years."

3. Six also refers to the number of steps in King Solomon's throne (1 Kings 10:19–20): "*Six* steps led up to the throne. . . . And twelve lions stood on the *six* steps, *six* on each side."

4. The winged, fiery angels in the Isaiah story had six wings (Isaiah 6:2): "Seraphim stood in attendance with Him. Each of them had *six* wings."

5. There was a six-cubit measuring reed in Ezekiel's vision (Ezekiel 40:5): "The rod that the man held was *six* cubits long."

6. "Ruth was given *six* measures of barley" (Ruth 3:15).

7. The number six also appears in reference to the architecture of the Tabernacle (Exodus 26:22): "And for the rear of the Tabernacle, to the west, make *six* planks."

The number sixty, which is a multiple of six, is dealt with in this volume in its own chapter.

THE NUMBER SIX IN RABBINIC THOUGHT

1. "*Six* things are a disgrace to an educated person: to walk on the street perfumed, to walk alone by night, to wear old clouted shoes, to walk with a woman overlong in the street, to sit at a table with illiterate men, and to be late at the synagogue" (Talmud *Berakhot* 43b).

2. "*Six* things are a certain cure for sickness: cabbage, beet root, water distilled from dry moss, the pancreas of an animal, and the lobe of the liver" (Talmud *Berakhot* 44b, 57b).

3. "There are *six* kinds of tears—three good, three bad. The bad ones are those caused by smoke, grief, constipation; the good ones are those caused by fragrant herbs, laughter, aromatic spices" (Talmud *Shabbat* 151b, 152a).

4. "Of *six* human characteristics, three are angelic and three are beastly. Human beings have intelligence, walk erect, and speak in the holy tongue like angels. They eat and drink, generate and multiply, and relive nature like animals" (Talmud *Chagigah* 16a).

5. "The horse is distinguished by *six* characteristics: it is wanton, delights in the strife of war, is high spirited, despises sleep, eats much, and voids little" (Talmud *Pesachim* 13b).

6. "God said of Esau: All things that I hate, he loves, as it is said:

Six things God hates;
Seven are an abomination to Him:
A haughty bearing,
A lying tongue,
Hands that shed blood of the innocent,
A mind that hatches evil plots,
Feet quick to run to evil,
A false witness testifying lies,
And one who incites brothers to quarrel." (*Midrash on Psalms* 14:3)

7. "Our masters taught: *Six* things were enjoined concerning the *am ha-aretz:* we may not ask him to act as a witness; we may not accept testimony from him; we may not reveal a secret to him; we may not appoint him as a guardian for orphans; we may not appoint him supervisor of charity funds; and we may not attach ourselves to him on the road" (Talmud *Pesachim* 49b).

8. "Rabbi Levi said: *Six* organs serve a man—three are under his control and three are not under his control. The ones under his control are the mouth, the hands, and the feet. The ones not under his control are the eyes, the ears, and the nose. And when the Holy One wishes it, even the ones under his control cease to be under it" (*Midrash Genesis Rabbah* 67:3).

THE NUMBER SIX IN JEWISH LIFE

The following is a summary of the number six as it appears in Jewish life.

1. Six days of creation.
2. Six cities of refuge.
3. Six sections of the Mishnah: *Zeraim, Moed, Nashim, Nezikin, Kodashim,* and *Tohorot.*
4. Six steps leading up to the throne of King Solomon.
5. Six chapters in the *Ethics of the Fathers*.

THE NUMBER SEVEN

THE NUMBER SEVEN IN THE BIBLE

The number seven played a very important role in ancient times. Indeed, the Bible mentions this number well over five hundred times! It was a sacred number to many peoples of the Ancient Near East, including the Assyrians, Egyptians, and Persians. It has been said that its importance is due in part to the worship of the seven heavenly bodies: the moon, the sun, and the five planets. Some also see the number seven as being composed of a combination of the sacred numbers three and four. Finally, there are some biblical scholars who suggest that the entire Book of Genesis and even the Five Books of Moses themselves are elaborately constructed around the sacred number seven.

In Mesopotamia the number seven was an ominous number. The seventh, fourteenth, twenty-first, and twenty-eighth days of each month were unlucky, and every forty-ninth day (seven times seven) was called the day of wrath.

Of all the numbers, the number seven was the most significant to the Hebrews. Because the creation of the world had required seven days, seven has come to symbolize completion and perfection. Indeed, the number seven as it appears in the Bible is connected with every aspect of religious life in almost every time frame. The following is a sampling of the presence of the number seven as it appears in biblical life.

1. The world is created in six days, and on the seventh day, God rests (Genesis 2:2ff.): "On the *seventh* day God finished the work that He had been doing, and He ceased on the *seventh* day from all the work that He had done. And God blessed the *seventh* day and declared it holy."

2. In the story of Noah (Genesis 7:2ff.): "Of every clean animal you shall take *seven* pairs, males and their mates."

3. Abraham makes a covenant with Avimelech (Genesis 21:28–30): "Abraham then set *seven* ewes of the flock by themselves, and Avimelech said to Abraham, 'What mean these *seven* ewes which you have set apart?' He replied, 'You are to accept these *seven* ewes from me as proof that I dug this well.' "

4. Cleansing from the dreaded biblical disease known as leprosy (Leviticus 14:9): "On the *seventh* day he shall shave off all his hair, he shall wash his clothes and bathe his body in water; then he shall be clean."

5. The biblical Festivals (Leviticus 23:8): "*Seven* days you shall make offerings by fire to God. The *seventh* day shall be a sacred occasion. You shall not work at your occupations."

6. Bilaam's altars (Numbers 23:1ff.): Bilaam said to Balak, "Build me *seven* altars and have *seven* bulls and *seven* rams ready here for me."

7. Sacrifices (Numbers 28:11): "On your new moons you shall present a burnt offering to God: two bulls of the herd, one ram, and *seven* yearling lambs, without blemish."

8. Temple furnishings (1 Kings 7:17): "Nets of meshwork with festoons of chainwork for the capitals that were on top of the columns, *seven* for each of the two capitals."

9. The menorah (candelabrum) that stood in the ancient tabernacle (Zechariah 4:2): "The lamps on it are *seven* in number, and the lamps above it have *seven* pipes."

10. Sprinkling of blood (Leviticus 4:6): "The priest shall dip his finger in the blood and sprinkle of the blood *seven* times before the Lord."

11. The mystical power of seven (Joshua 6:4, 8, 13): "With *seven* priests . . . carrying *seven* ram's horns preceding the Ark. On the *seventh* day, march around the city *seven* times, with the priests blowing the horns. . . . When Joshua had instructed the people, the *seven* priests carrying *seven* ram's horns advanced before God, blowing their horns."

12. Punishments:

If Cain is avenged *sevenfold,* then Lamech *sevenfold.* (Genesis 4:24)

And if, for all that, you do not obey Me, I will go on to discipline you *sevenfold* for your sins. (Leviticus 26:18)

Let his mind be altered from that of man, and let him be given the mind of a beast, and let *seven* seasons pass over him. (Daniel 4:13)

13. Time periods:

He waited another *seven* days, and again sent out the dove from the ark. (Genesis 8:10)

When *seven* days had passed after God struck the Nile, the Lord said to Moses . . . (Exodus 7:25)

On the *seventh* day, they rose at daybreak and marched around the city, in the same manner, *seven* times; that was the only day that they marched around the city *seven* times. (Joshua 6:15)

14. Marriage:

So Jacob served *seven* years for Rachel and they seemed to him but a few days because of his love for her. (Genesis 29:20)

Then Samson said to them, "Let me propound a riddle to you. If you can give me the right answer during the *seven* days of the feast, I shall give you thirty tunics of clothing." (Judges 14:12)

15. Famine and plenty:

Elisha had said to the woman whose son he revived, "Leave immediately with your family and go sojourn somewhere else, for the Lord has decreed a *seven*-year famine upon the land." (2 Kings 8:1)

Let Pharaoh take steps to appoint overseers over the land and organize the land of Egypt in the *seven* years of plenty. (Genesis 41:34)

16. Prostrations (Genesis 33:3): "He himself went on ahead and bowed low to the ground *seven* times until he was near his brother."

17. The half of seven, three and a half, also has special significance (Daniel 9:27): "During one week he will make a firm covenant with many. For half a week [i.e., *three and a half days*], he will put a stop to the sacrifice and the meal offering."

18. Number seven represents a complete, round number of moderate size:

> In that day, *seven* women shall take hold of one man. (Isaiah 4:1)

> Should Assyria invade our land and tread upon our fortresses, we will set up over it *seven* shepherds. (Micah 5:4)

> On the *seventh* day, when the king was merry with wine, he ordered . . . (Esther 1:10)

19. Multiples of seven are generally used as numbers allowing for added emphasis (Leviticus 12:5): "If she bears a female, [she] shall be unclean for two weeks [i.e., *two times seven days*] as during her menstruation." (For a discussion on the number 70, see that chapter.)

THE NUMBER SEVEN IN RABBINIC THOUGHT

The number seven appears numerous times in rabbinic thought. Here is a sampling of these references to the number seven.

1. "*Seven* attributes help to bring a person nearer to the Throne of Glory: wisdom, righteousness, judgment, grace, mercy, truth, and peace" (*Avot de Rabbi Natan* 36:5).

2. "*Seven* lights were created before the universe came into being: the light of Torah, the light of Paradise, the light of Gehenna, the light of the Throne of Glory, the light of the Holy Temple, the light of penitence, and the light of the Messiah" (*Zohar* III:31a).

3. "*Seven* things are hidden from the knowledge of man: the day of death, the day of relief from troubles, the depth of eternal justice, the future reward or punishment, that which is in his fellowman's heart, the restoration of the kingdom of David, and the date of the fall of the kingdom of Persia" (Talmud *Pesachim* 54b).

4. "The *seven* shepherds mentioned in Amos 5:5 are Adam, Seth, Methusaleh, David, Abraham, Jacob, and Moses" (Talmud *Sukkah* 52b).

5. The *seven* prophetesses were Sarah, Miriam, Deborah, Channah, Abigail, Chuldah, and Esther.

6. "Moses was born and died on the *seventh* day of the month of Adar, and it was on this day as well that the manna ceased to fall" (Talmud *Megillah* 13b).

7. "There are *seven* stages of transgression: evil thought, scoffing, arrogance, cruelty, idleness, causeless hatred, and malevolence" (Talmud *Derech Eretz Zutah* 6).

8. "*Seven* men form an unbroken chain from Creation to our own time: Methusaleh saw Adam; Shem saw Methusaleh; Jacob saw Shem; Amram saw Jacob; Ahijah the Shilonite saw Amran; and Ahijah was seen by Elijah the Prophet who, according to tradition, is still alive" (Talmud *Bava Batra* 121b).

9. "While a ram has but one voice while alive, it has *seven* voices after its death: its horns make two trumpets, its leg bones make two flutes, its skin makes a drum, its

larger intestines yield strings for the lyre, its smaller ones yield strings for the harp'' (Mishnah *Kinnim* 3:6).

10. ''*Seven* children were born circumcised: Adam, Seth, Noah, Jacob, Joseph, Moses, and Job'' *(Midrash Tanchuma, Noach).*

11. ''There are *seven* marks of the uncultured and *seven* of the wise person. The wise person does not speak before one that is greater than he in wisdom; he does not break in upon the words of his fellow; he is not hasty in making answers; he asks only what is relevant and answers to the point; he speaks on the first thing first and on the last thing last, and of what he has heard no tradition, he says: 'I have not heard'; and he agrees to what is true, and the opposite of these are the marks of the uncultured'' (*Ethics of the Fathers* 5:10).

12. ''*Seven* kinds of punishment come upon this world for *seven* classes of transgression. If some give their tithes and others do not, there comes famine from drought: some suffer hunger while others have enough'' (*Ethics of the Fathers* 5:11).

13. ''There are *seven* characteristics in an uncultured man and *seven* in a wise man. A wise man does not speak before one who is greater than he in wisdom, does not enter in the midst of the words of his fellow, is not hasty to answer; he asks in accordance with the subject matter and answers in accordance with the accepted decision, speaks on the first point first and on the last point last; concerning what he has not heard he says, 'I have not heard it,' and acknowledges the truth. The reverse of these are in an uncultured person'' (Talmud *Derech Eretz Zutah* 58b).

14. "The following *seven* patriarchs have gone to their eternal rest with great honor and worms and maggots had not dominion over them: Abraham, Isaac, Jacob, Moses, Aaron, Miriam, and their father Amram" (Talmud *Derech Eretz Zutah* 58a).

15. "There were *seven* patriarchs with whom a Divine covenant was made: Abraham, Isaac, Jacob, Moses, Aaron, Phinehas, and David. In connection with Abraham it is written, 'In that day God made a covenant with Abraham, saying, "In connection with Isaac it is written, 'But My covenant will I establish with Isaac.' In connection with Jacob it is written, 'Then will I remember My covenant with Jacob.' In connection with Moses it is written, 'For after the tenor of these words I have made a covenant with you and with Israel.' In connection with Aaron it is written, 'It is an everlasting covenant of salt before God.' In connection with Phinehas it is written, 'And it shall be unto him and to his seed after him, the covenant of an everlasting priesthood.' In connection with David it is written, 'I have made a covenant with My chosen, I have sworn unto David My servant' '' ' '' (Talmud *Derech Eretz Zutah* 57b–58a).

16. "*Seven* things were created before the world was created: Torah, repentance, the Garden of Eden, Gehenna, the throne of glory, the Temple, and the name of the Messiah" (Talmud *Pesachim* 54a).

17. "*Seven* are as if under heaven's ban: a man who has no wife; who has a wife but no children; who has children but does not rear them in the study of Torah; who has no *tefillin* on the head and arm, no fringes on his garment, no mezuzah at the entrance of his house, and who denies shoes to his feet" (Talmud *Pesachim* 113b).

18. "Rabbi Huna said: As a remedy for tertian fever, one should procure *seven* prickles from *seven* date palms, *seven* chips from *seven* beams, *seven* pegs from *seven* bridges, *seven* handfuls of ash from *seven* ovens, *seven* pinches of earth from *seven* graves, *seven* bits of pitch from *seven* ships, *seven* seeds of cumin, and *seven* hairs from the beard of an old dog, and tie them inside the collar of his shirt with a band of twined strands of wool" (Talmud *Shabbat* 67a).

THE NUMBER SEVEN IN JEWISH LIFE

Here is a summary of the various places in Jewish life where the number seven plays a role.

1. Seven blessings in the *Amidah* of *Shabbat* and Jewish holidays.
2. Seven processionals around the *bimah* on the holidays of Hoshanna Rabbah and Simchat Torah.
3. Seven years comprise the year of letting one's land lie fallow (i.e., the sabbatical year).
4. There are seven wedding blessings chanted under the wedding canopy.
5. The omer is counted for a period of seven weeks.
6. The bride and groom are to rejoice for seven days according to Jewish law.
7. Seven times Naaman immersed himself in the Jordan to be cured of leprosy.
8. Seven sons of Channah were killed for the sanctification of God's Name.
9. There were seven woman prophets of Israel.
10. There are seven days in the initial period of Jewish mourning.

11. There are seven lights on the menorah in the Temple.
12. Jacob worked seven years in order to acquire Rachel as his wife.
13. There were seven years of plenty in Egypt.
14. Phylacteries (*tefillin*) are wrapped seven times around one's arm.
15. The minimum size of a *sukkah* is seven *tefachim* (one *tefachim* is the width of a clenched fist) by seven *tefachim*.
16. Seven biblical species (Deuteronomy 8:8) include: wheat, barley, vines, figs, pomegranates, olive trees, and honey.

THE NUMBER EIGHT

THE NUMBER EIGHT IN THE BIBLE

The number eight appears in the Bible but nowhere to the extent of the symbolic number seven. Here are the highlights of the appearance of the number eight.

1. Circumcision (Genesis 17:12): "Throughout the generations, every male among you shall be circumcised at the age of *eight* days."

2. Consecration of firstborn animals (Exodus 22:29): "You shall do the same with your cattle and your flocks: seven days it shall remain with its mother; on the *eighth* day you shall give it to Me."

3. Sacrifices (Numbers 6:10): "On the *eighth* day he shall bring two turtledoves or two pigeons to the priest, at the entrance of the Tent of Meeting."

4. Holy Convocation (Leviticus 23:36): "On the *eighth* day you shall observe a sacred celebration and bring an offering by fire to God."

5. Temple structure (Ezekiel 40:31): "Its supports were adorned on either side with palms, and its staircase consisted of *eight* steps."

THE NUMBER EIGHT IN RABBINIC THOUGHT

1. "Of *eight* things a little is good and much is evil:
travel, mating, wealth, work, wine, sleep, hot drinks,
and medicine" (Talmud *Gittin* 70).

2. "*Eight* additional letters point the way toward the
use of decent language. When God commanded Noah
to take the animals into the ark, instead of saying 'unclean,' which has an indecent connotation, He said,
'those which are not clean [Genesis 7:2, 8],' thereby
employing additional letters to avoid indecency" (Talmud *Pesachim* 3a).

3. "The last *eight* verses of the Torah, according to
one tradition, were written by Joshua, and according to
another by Moses himself, at the Almighty's dictation"
(Talmud *Bava Batra* 15a).

4. "There are *eight* things that are harmful in excess
but beneficial in limited quantity: travel, intercourse,
accumulation of wealth, strenuous labor, wine, sleep,
hot baths, bloodletting" (Talmud *Gittin* 70a).

5. "Because of *eight* things is the world destroyed:
injustice in the courts, idolatry, incest, murder, profana-
tion of God's Name, because of foul things a person
utters, arrogance, and the evil tongue" (*Seder Eliahu,*
ed. M. Friedmann [Vienna, 1900], 74).

6. The *eight* names of the poor are "Ani" derived
from "Ane," to afflict. "Ebion" derived from "Aba," to
want. "Misken" derived from "Masken," impoverished.
"Rash" derived from "Tiwaresh," landless. "Dal" derived from "Meduldal," empty-handed. "Dak" derived
from "Medukdak," beaten down. "Mak" derived from
"Yamuk," reduced low. And "Halek" derived from

"Halok," to wander about *(Midrash Leviticus Rabbah, Behar)*.

THE NUMBER EIGHT IN JEWISH LIFE

The following are some of the ways in which the number eight plays a role in various aspects of Jewish life:

1. Eight days of Chanukah.
2. A male child is eight days old when circumcised.
3. There are eight strands on the end of each prayer shawl fringe.
4. Jesse, King David's father, had eight sons.
5. An animal in biblical times was to be with its mother for eight days before it could be sacrificed.
6. There were eight different garments to be worn by the High Priest.
7. Outside of Israel, the Festival of Passover is celebrated for a period of eight days.
8. Maimonides identified eight degrees of *tzedakah,* or charity *(Mishneh Torah):*
    i. The person who gives reluctantly and with regret.
    ii. The person who gives graciously but less than he should.
    iii. The person who gives what he should, but only after being asked.
    iv. The person who gives before being asked.
    v. The person who gives without knowing to whom he gives, although the recipient knows the identity of the donor.
    vi. The person who gives without making his identity known.

vii. The person who gives without knowing to
whom he gives. The recipient does not know
from whom he receives.

viii. The person who helps another to support
himself by a gift or a loan or by finding
employment for that person, thus helping him
to become self-supporting.

THE NUMBER TEN

THE NUMBER TEN IN THE BIBLE

Like the number five, the number ten seems to be derived from the use of the fingers in counting. It is the basis of the numeral system that is chiefly, though not solely, used in the Bible. It expresses completeness and perfection, and its sacred character may, in fact, be derived from the fact that it is the product of three and seven (both sacred numbers). The fraction one-tenth formed the tithe.

Here are some examples of the number ten as they appear in the Bible. (There are a number of multiples of ten throughout the Bible, which will be illustrated in separate chapters.)

Ten Expressing Completeness

1. "Then the servant took *ten* of his master's camels and set out, taking with him all the bounty of his master. When the camels had finished drinking, the man took a gold nose ring weighing half of a shekel, and two gold bands for her arms, *ten* shekels in weight" (Genesis 24:10, 22).

2. "And *ten* princes with him, one prince each for every division of all the tribes of Israel" (Joshua 22:14).

3. "And Micah said to him: Remain with me and become for me a father and a priest, and I will give you *ten* shekels of silver for the year" (Judges 17:10–11).

4. "And Isaiah said: This shall be the sign from God, that the Lord will do the thing that he has spoken: Shall the shadow go forward *ten* degrees, or go backward *ten* degrees? And Hezekiah said, It is a light thing for the shadow to go forward *ten* degrees: no, but let the shadow return backward *ten* degrees. And Isaiah the prophet called to God, and He caused the shadow to return, by the degrees that the sun was gone down on the dial of Achaz, backward, *ten* degrees" (2 Kings 20:9–11).

5. "But *ten* men were found among them that said to Ishmael, Slay us not" (Jeremiah 41:8).

6. "These *ten* times have you reproached me" (Job 19:3).

7. "And he said, Let not the Lord be angry, and I will speak yet but this once: Peradventure there will be found there *ten*. And God said, I will not destroy, for the sake of *ten*" (Genesis 18:32).

Ten Expressing the Concept of the Tithe

"When you take from the children of Israel the tithes which I have given you from them for your inheritance, then shall you separate therefrom a heave-offering of God, the *tenth* part of the tithe" (Numbers 18:26).

Ten as It Occurs in the Bible in Latent Form

1. There are ten patriarchs from Adam to Noah (Genesis 5): Adam, Seth, Enosh, Kenan, Mechalalel, Jared, Enoch, Methusaleh, Lamech, and Noah.

2. There were ten persons from the generation of Noah to that of Abraham (Genesis 11:27): Shem, Arpachshad, Shelach, Eber, Peleg, Reu, Serug, Hachor, Terach, and Abraham.

3. The Israelites put God to the test ten times (Numbers 14:22): "Surely all those men that have seen My glory, and My signs, which I have wrought in Egypt and in the wilderness, yet have put Me to proof these *ten* times, and have not hearkened to My voice."

4. In ritual observances the fraction one-tenth occurs frequently.

And the *tenth* part of an ephah of fine flour for a meal offering. (Numbers 28:5)

And three *tenth* parts of an ephah of fine flour for a meal offering, mingled with oil, for each bullock; and two *tenth* parts of fine flour for a meal offering, mingled with oil, for the one ram. (Numbers 28:12)

And all the tithe of the herd or the flock, whatsoever passes under the rod, the *tenth* shall be holy unto God. (Leviticus 27:32)

And when the matter was spread abroad, the children of Israel brought in abundance the first fruits of corn, of the new wine, and of oil, and of honey, and of all the products of the field. And the *tithe* (i.e., *tenth*) of all things did they bring likewise in abundance. (2 Chronicles 31:5)

Bring all the *tithes* (i.e., *tenths*) into the storehouse, that there may be provision in my house. (Malachi 3:10)

The Ten Commandments

According to the Bible, there were ten Divine laws spoken by God to Moses and written on two tablets of stone. They appear in two slightly different forms in Exodus 20:2–17 and Deuteronomy 5:6–21.

1. I am Adonai your God, who brought you out of the land of Egypt, out of the house of bondage.
2. You shall have no other gods in place of Me, nor make for yourself any idols.
3. You shall not speak God's Name for no purpose.
4. Remember the Sabbath Day and keep it holy.
5. Honor your father and mother.
6. Do not murder.
7. Do not commit adultery.
8. Do not steal.
9. Do not bear false witness against your neighbor.
10. Do not covet anything that your neighbor owns.

The Ten Plagues

According to the Bible, there were ten afflictions suffered by the Egyptians as a result of Pharaoh's refusal to permit the Israelites to leave the country (Exodus 7:14–12:34). These plagues are recited aloud during the Passover seder meal.

Blood
Frogs

Lice
Flies
Cattle disease
Boils
Heavy hail
Locusts
Darkness
Death of the firstborn

THE NUMBER TEN IN RABBINIC THOUGHT

The number ten plays a prominent role in rabbinic thought. It is an especially prominent number in the rabbinic tractate, *Ethics of the Fathers*, and is also the most significant number in Jewish mysticism as it seeks to explain the transition from the Infinite Cause of Causes (i.e., God), called the *"Ein Sof,"* to the tangible universe, by means of ten graded emanations (called *sefirot*) representing the forms into which all created things were originally cast.

Here are some illustrations of the number ten and the part that it plays in rabbinic literature.

1. According to rabbinic thought (*Ethics of the Fathers* 5:9), there were ten things that were created on the eve of the Sabbath at dusk. They include:

1. The mouth of the earth that swallowed up Korach and his followers.
2. The mouth of the well that supplied the Israelites with water while they traveled through the desert.
3. The mouth of Bilaam's donkey that spoke.
4. The rainbow that was shown to Noah at the end of the flood.

5. The manna that came from heaven to feed the Israelites while they wandered through the wilderness.
6. The staff that Moses used.
7. The *shamir* (a worm that had the power of splitting the hardest stone) that King Solomon used to build the Jerusalem Temple.
8. The forms of the letters that were engraved in the tablets of the Ten Commandments.
9. The writing on the Ten Commandment tablets which were able to be read from all four sides.
10. The first tablets of the Ten Commandments.

2. There are ten *kal v'chomers* that are mentioned in the Torah. A *kal v'chomer* is an a fortiori argument, a fundamental principle of rabbinic exegesis. It is a rule of logical argumentation by means of which two cases are compared, one lenient and the other more stringent. The *kav v'chomer* principle asserts that if the law is stringent in a case where we are usually lenient, then it will certainly be stringent in a more serious case.

Here are the ten *kal v'chomers*, as presented in *Genesis Rabbah* (portion of *Mikketz*).

i. The ten brothers of Joseph replied to the servant who overtook them and accused them of stealing the goblet of Joseph: "Behold, the money we found at the top of our sacks we returned to you. Does it not, then, stand to reason: 'How would we steal the goblet of your master?' " (Genesis 44:7–8).

ii. When God told Moses to go to Pharaoh and tell him to let the Jews out so that they might serve God, Moses remarked: "Behold, the Jewish people did not listen to me. [They should have listened more than

anyone else, so why should Pharaoh listen to me?]''
(Exodus 6:12).

iii. Moses gathered the children of Israel all together
before his death, and among the things he spoke to
them, he said: ''Behold, while I am yet alive with you,
you have been rebellious against God. How much more
so will it be after my death?'' (Deuteronomy 31:27).

iv. When God was talking to Moses about the punishment of Miriam, He said: ''Had her father spit in her
face, surely it would stand to reason that she would hide
in shame for seven days'' (Numbers 12:14).

v. God said to Jeremiah: ''If you have run with the
footmen, and they have made you tired, then how will
you be able to contend with the horses? [If your own
relatives wish to kill you, surely the princes of Judah,
who are not in any way related to you, would want to
kill you.]'' (Jeremiah 12:5).

vi. God continued to speak to Jeremiah and said: ''In
a land of peace where you are secure [i.e., Anatoth] and
yet they desire to kill you, then how will you do in the
high places of the Jordan? The princes will surely want
to kill you'' (Jeremiah 12:12).

vii. His men said to David: ''Behold, while you are in
Judah, among our own people we are afraid. Surely it
will be like that when we go to Keilah, where we will be
surrounded by Philistines'' (1 Samuel 23:3).

viii. King Solomon said: ''Why should the wicked
person feel so confident? He sees that the righteous
person is punished for the small amount of wrong-
doing. Surely it stands to reason that the wicked person
will be punished'' (Proverbs 11:31).

ix. And the king said to Queen Esther: "The Jews have killed five hundred men in Shushan. One can then imagine what they have done throughout the other provinces of the king" (Esther 9:12).

x. God said to Ezekiel: "Behold, while the wood was whole, it was not fitting for any work, since it was weak. Surely after it has been consumed by fire, and it is singed, can work be done with it?" (Ezekiel 15:15).

3. According to rabbinic thought (*Ethics of the Fathers* 5:8), there were *ten* miracles that were wrought for our ancestors in the Temple. They were:

    i. No woman miscarried from the scent of the holy meat.

    ii. The holy meat never turned putrid.

    iii. No fly was seen in the slaughterhouse.

    iv. No unclean accident ever happened to the High Priest on the Day of Atonement.

    v. The rain never quenched the fire on the woodpile on the altar.

    vi. No one prevailed over the column of smoke that arose from it.

    vii. There was never a defect found in the omer, in the two loaves, or in the shewbread.

    viii. The people stood pressed together yet bowed themselves at ease.

    ix. Never did a serpent or scorpion do harm in Jerusalem.

    x. No man said to his fellow person: "The place is too crowded for me [so] I should lodge in Jerusalem."

4. To bridge the gap between the unknowable God and the known universe, Jewish mysticism teaches that

between God and world are *ten sefirot*, Divine luminaries through which God is revealed. It is through these
sefirot that mystics believe the world came into being
and is preserved. The names of the *ten sefirot* are:

Keter (Crown)
Chochmah (Wisdom)
Binah (Understanding)
Chesed (Mercy)
Din or *Gevurah* (Judgment or Power)
Tiferet (Beauty)
Netzach (Eternity)
Hod (Majesty)
Yesod (Foundation)
Malchut (Kingdom)

5. As part of the penitential prayers of the Musaf
Additional Service, which is recited on the afternoon of
the Day of Atonement, the traditional prayer book includes a martyrology recording the death of *ten* rabbis
for the sanctification of God's Name. The events referred to took place during the Hadrianic persecution
following the year 135 c.e. The Talmud relates the tale
of the ten leading rabbis of Palestine who continued to
meet and determined, in defiance of the Roman authorities, that they would under no circumstances cease
teaching Torah. The fate meted out to them is graph-
ically described in this version of the story, which is
attributed to Rabbi Judah.

These things I do remember and my heart is grieved.
How the arrogant have devoured our people. In the
reign of a certain emperor, ten sages, though innocent,

were doomed to death by his command. The tyrant, searching our Torah for an excuse, yea a sword to slay us, found this law among the ordinances: "And he that steals a man and sells him, shall surely be put to death."

Elated, he summoned ten great sages of our Torah and put to them this question: "What is the law if a person is found stealing his brother, one of the children of Israel, and makes merchandise of him and sells him?"

And the sages instantly replied, "That thief shall die."

And the despot said, "They are your ancestors who sold their brother Joseph to the Ishmaelites. If they were living, I would pronounce sentence against them as you have spoken, but now you must bear your father's sin."

And that cruel oppressor commanded that the ten sages be slain. Two of the great in Israel were first brought forth to the slaughter, the High Priest, Rabbi Ishmael and Rabban Simeon ben Gamliel, the Prince, the ruler in Israel.

Then Rabban Simeon implored: "O, slay me lest you slay him, lest I see the death of him who ministered to God."

The tyrant bade them to cast lots, and the lot fell on Rabbi Simeon, who was immediately killed.

Rabbi Ishmael raised the severed head and bitterly cried out like a trumpet blast: "How is the tongue, skilled in the word of God, brought low to lick the dust."

And while he cried, the tyrant's daughter stood, and gazing upon the High Priest's handsome features, implored her father to spare his life, but her father refused to do so. They began to flay off the skin from Rabbi Ishmael's face.

(Terror makes me dumb so that I cannot describe the tortures that my eyes beheld.)

Even the seraphim in the heights of the heaven called out in anguish: "Is this then the reward for the Torah, You, who spreads out light as a garment? The enemy blasphemes Your great Name and scorns Your Law."

But out of heaven's height, a voice replied, "The way to truth and justice is often filled with affliction and pain."

Thus were the princes of the Law slain: Rabbi Akiba, the greatest of them all, whose flesh they tore with a sharp instrument, and Rabbi Chananya, son of Tera-dyon, whom they burned with the parchment of the Sefer Torah wrapped about him.

Mourn, O my people; because of the cruel whim of tyrants, our sages were slaughtered for the sake of God.

Men like Chuzpit, the Interpreter, willingly suffered martyrdom.

Trembling takes hold of all who hear, and tears flow from all eyes, and all delight is dead for the murder of a sage like Eliezer, son of Shamua.

How have our enemies fed on us. How do they give us water of gall and hemlock to drink. For they slew Chanina, son of Chakinai.

They tortured us that we might break the commandments; they refused to take ransom but insisted on the lives of those who studied Torah, such as the Scribe Yeshevav.

The sons of voluptuousness make us desolate. They have oppressed us more than the kings of earth. They have slain numbers of us, among them, Judah, son of Dama.

It is written in Your Torah: "Jacob shall be a fire, Joseph a flame, and the house of Esau, stubble," but now the stubble has quenched the fire.

O bring near the day of reckoning, for Judah, son of Baba, was not spared. Thus were *ten* righteous men slain. (Martyrology Service of Yom Kippur)

6. *"Ten* things cause hemorrhoids: cane leaves, tendrils of the vine, foliage of the vine, the palate of cattle, the backbones of fish, half-cooked salted fish, lees of wine, wiping with three injurious, irritating substances" (Talmud *Berakhot* 55a).

7. *"Ten* things lead to a convalescent's relapse: eating beef, fat meat, broiled meat, flesh of birds, roasted eggs; shaving; eating cress; drinking milk; eating cheese; a full bath. Some sages also include eating nuts, and others add cucumbers" (Talmud *Berakhot* 57b).

8. "If there are *ten* men of leisure who are able to attend the synagogue at any time in a place, it is large enough to be called a town; otherwise it is considered a village" (Talmud *Megillah* 3b).

9. *"Ten* terms are used to denote a prophet: ambassador, faithful, servant, messenger, seer, watchman, seer of vision, dreamer, prophet, man of God" (*Avot de Rabbi Natan* 34).

10. *"Ten* things were created during twilight at the first Sabbath eve: the well that accompanied the Israelites through the wilderness; manna; the rainbow; the shape of the written characters; the art of writing; the two Tables of stone on which the Ten Commandments were engraved; the grave of Moses; the cave in which Moses and Elijah stayed; the speech of Bilaam's donkey; the opening of the earth that engulfed Korach and his followers. To which some add Aaron's staff

which blossomed, the destroying spirits, and Adam's garments'' (Talmud *Pesachim* 54a).

11. "King David included in the Book of Psalms those composed by *ten* elders: Adam (Psalm 139); Melchizedek (110); Abraham (59); Moses (90); those of Heman, Jeduthun, and Asaph; and those of the three sons of Korach" (Talmud *Bava Batra* 14b, 15a).

12. "*Ten* things of strength were created, but that which follows them is stronger: a mountain is strong, but iron hews it in pieces; fire weakens iron; water quenches fire; the clouds carry off water; the wind disperses the clouds; the living body resists the wind; fear enervates the body; wine abolishes fear; sleep overcomes wine; and death overpowers them all" (Talmud *Bava Batra* 10a).

13. "Manifestation of the Holy Spirit is described in *ten* ways: proverb, interpretation, riddle, saying, oracle, glory, decree, burden, prophecy, vision" (*Avot de Rabbi Natan* 34).

14. "*Ten* individuals coveted that to which they were not entitled, and they did not achieve it: the serpent, Cain, Korach, Bilaam, Achithophel, Doeg, Absalom, Adoniyahu, Uzziahu, Gechazzi" (*Chuppat Eliyahu, Otzar Midrashim* 177).

15. "With *ten* temptations was Abraham our father tempted, and he stood firm in all of them, to show how great was the love of Abraham our father" (*Ethics of the Fathers* 5:4).

16. "*Ten* songs are mentioned in Scripture. The first, which was sung in Egypt, 'You shall have a song, as in the night of the first Passover when a feast was hallowed

[Isaiah 30:29].' The second, which was sung at the Red Sea, 'Then sang Moses [Exodus 15:1].' The third, which was chanted at the well: 'Then sang Israel [Numbers 21:17].' The fourth, which Moses uttered: 'So Moses wrote this song [Deuteronomy 31:22].' The fifth, which Joshua recited: 'Then spoke Joshua to God [Joshua 10:12].' The sixth, which Deborah and Barak uttered: 'Then sang Deborah and Barak the son of Abinoam [Judges 5:1].' The seventh, which David recited: 'And David spoke to God the words of this song [2 Samuel 22:1].' The eighth, which Solomon recited: 'Then spoke Solomon [2 Chronicles 6:1].' The ninth, which Jehoshaphat uttered: 'And when he had taken counsel with the people, he appointed them that should sing to God, and praise to the beauty of holiness [2 Chronicles 20:21].' The tenth song will be recited in the time to come: 'Sing to God a new song, and God's praise from the end of the earth [Isaiah 42:10]' '' (*Yalkut, BeShallach,* par. 254).

17.

Ten kav of wealth descended to the world: the Romans took nine, and all the rest of the world one.

Ten kav of poverty descended to the world: Babylon took nine, and all the rest of the world one.

Ten kav of presumptuousness descended to the world: Elam took nine, and all the rest of the world one.

Ten kav of might descended to the world: the Persians took nine, and all the rest of the world one.

Ten kav of witchcraft descended to the world; Egypt took nine, and all the rest of the world one.

Ten kav of harlotry descended to the world: Arabia took nine, and all the rest of the world one.

Ten kav of impudence descended to the world: Mesene took nine, and all the rest of the world one.
Ten kav of drunkenness descended to the world: the Ethiopians took nine, and all the rest of the world one. (Talmud *Kiddushin* 49b)

18.

There are *ten* portions of stupidity in the world—nine among the Ishmaelites and one in the rest of the world.
There are *ten* portions of outlawry in the world—nine among the Ishmaelites and *one* in the rest of the world.
There are *ten* portions of physical beauty in the world—nine in Media and one in the rest of the world.
There are *ten* portions of ugliness in the world—nine in the east and one in the rest of the world.
There are *ten* portions of physical strength in the world—nine among the Chaldeans and one in the rest of the world. (Talmud *Esther Rabbah* 1:17)

19. "*Ten* things serve the soul: the gullet for food, the windpipe for voice, the liver for temper, the lungs to absorb liquids, the first stomach to grind food, the spleen for laughter, the maw for sleep, the gallbladder for jealousy, the kidneys for thought, and the heart for decision making" (*Midrash Leviticus Rabbah* 4:4).

20. "Before you eat your piece of bread, remember that *ten mitzvot* have been performed in preparing it for your consumption: it was not sown on the Sabbath day or Sabbath year, it was not plowed then, the ox's mouth was not tied while he worked in the field, the grower has not gathered the leftover and forgotten sheaves, he has not reaped the ends of the field, he has

given the *terumah* and the tithe to the Levi, the second tithe and the tithe of the poor has he given. And your wife has separated a piece of the dough as challah for the *Kohen*'' (Jerusalem Talmud, *Challah* 1).

21. ''*Ten* special regulations were applied to Jerusalem. Among them that no dunghills were to be made there; that no kilns were to be kept there; that neither gardens nor orchards were allowed to be cultivated there aside from the rose gardens that existed from the days of the early prophets; that no chickens may be raised there; and that no dead persons may be kept there overnight'' (Talmud *Bava Kamma* 82b).

22. ''We read in *Ethics of the Fathers* 5:1: 'With *ten* sayings the world was created.' This number is taken in order to correspond to the Decalogue.

''The first saying: 'Let there be light,' corresponds to the First commandment; for we remember that God is the Eternal Light.

''The second: 'Let there be an expanse,' reminds us that all heavenly bodies are creatures only.

''The third: 'Let the waters assemble,' reminds us that the water of the sea does not hold lightly the Name of God, and does not overflow its bounds.

''The fourth: 'Let the earth bring forth grass,' reminds us of God's bounty to him who honors the Sabbath.

''The fifth; 'Let there be lights,' reminds us of two other lights in the life of man, namely, his father and mother. If he honors them he will walk in light next to the Eternal Light.

''The sixth: 'Let the waters bring forth fowl, etc.,' reminds us that we may slay these creatures for our use, but not men.

"The seventh: 'Let the earth bring forth creatures after their own kind,' reminds us that only beasts may multiply promiscuously, but man must not commit adultery.

"The eighth: 'Let us make man . . . who shall have dominion,' reminds us that man should make use only of that over which he has dominion. He should not steal, however, that over which others have dominion.

"The ninth: 'I have given . . . every tree on which is the fruit,' reminds us that as the tree fulfills its function truly, so should man's lips fulfil their function by speaking the truth.

"The tenth: 'It is not good that man should be alone,' reminds us that just as Adam did not covet another's wife, we also should not covet" (*Pesikta Hadrashah, Otzar Midrashim,* 491).

23. "*Ten* things adversely affect one's capacity to learn: passing under a camel's bit, passing between two camels, passing between two women, a woman passing beneath two men, passing within smelling distance of a decaying carcass, passing under a bridge beneath which no water has flowed for forty days, eating bread insufficiently baked, eating meat out of a soup ladle, drinking from a water channel that runs through a graveyard, and looking into the face of a dead body" (Talmud *Horayot* 13b).

THE NUMBER TEN IN JEWISH LIFE

Here is a summary of the number ten and its prominence in Jewish life:

1. Ten people constitute a quorum (i.e., a minyan).
2. Ten commandments.

3. Ten generations from Adam until Noah.
4. Ten generations from Noah until Abraham.
5. Ten tests that God gave Abraham to test his faith.
6. Ten tribes comprised the kingdom of Israel after the death of King Solomon.
7. Ten brothers of Joseph who came to Egypt to buy food the first time.
8. The ten plagues (blood, frogs, lice, flies, cattle disease, boils, hail, locusts, darkness, and death of the firstborn son).
9. Ten mystical *sefirot* (crown, wisdom, intelligence, loving-kindness, power, beauty, eternity, majesty, foundation, and kingdom).
10. Ten sons of Haman (Parshandata, Dalphon, Aspatha, Poratha, Adalia, Aridatha, Parmashta, Arisai, Aridai, and Vaizatha).
11. Ten *kal v'chomers* in the Torah (i.e., a fortiori arguments, or conclusions, drawn from a minor premise or more lenient condition to a major or more strict condition, and vice versa).

THE NUMBER TWELVE

THE NUMBER TWELVE IN THE BIBLE

Many symbolic numbers in the Ancient Near East were derived from astrological calculations based on the worship of the sun and moon in Mesopotamia and Egypt. A zodiac of twelve signs, for instance, was invented in Mesopotamia before 2000 B.C.E., and the year was divided into twelve lunar months in both Mesopotamia and Palestine. Because of its astrological significance, twelve became an important number in the Bible. Here are some references to the biblical number twelve.

1.   Twelve tribes of Israel (Genesis 35:22): "Now the sons of Jacob were *twelve* in number."

2.   Tribes of Ishmael (Genesis 17:20): "As for Ishmael, I have heeded you and hereby bless him. I will make him fertile and exceedingly numerous, and he shall be the father of *twelve* chieftains."

3.   Representative persons and objects:

Early in the morning, Moses set up an altar at the foot of the mountain, with *twelve* pillars for the *twelve* tribes of Israel. (Exodus 24:4)

You shall take choice flour and bake of it *twelve* loaves. (Leviticus 24:5)

Six draught cars and *twelve* oxen, a cart for every two chieftains and an ox for each one. (Numbers 7:3)

Select *twelve* men from among the people, one from each tribe. (Joshua 4:2)

And *twelve* lions stood on the six steps, six on either side. (1 Kings 10:20)

And they sacrificed for the dedication of the House of God one hundred bulls, two hundred rams, four hundred lambs, and *twelve* goats as a purification offering for all of Israel. (Ezra 6:17)

The number twelve also appears as a latent number in the Bible. For instance, the male descendants of Adam listed in Genesis 4:1–26 numbered twelve, and the verb *yalad* ("to bear") occurs there twelve times.

There are also several examples of multiples of twelve in the Bible, which will be presented in separate chapters.

THE NUMBER TWELVE IN RABBINIC THOUGHT

The number twelve appears throughout rabbinic thought. Here is a sampling.

1. "The day consists of *twelve* hours, and that was the length of time Adam spent in the Garden of Eden. During the first hour, dust was collected from all parts of the world; during the second it was made into a

lump; during the third his limbs were formed; during the fourth his body was animated; the fifth, he stood upon his legs; the sixth, he gave names to the animals; the seventh, he associated with Eve; the eighth, Cain and a twin sister were born; the ninth, he was ordered not to eat of the forbidden tree; the tenth, he succumbed to temptation; the eleventh, he was judged; during the twelfth, he was banished from Eden" (Talmud *Sanhedrin* 38b).

2. "A creature that has no bones in its body does not live more than *twelve* months" (Talmud *Chullin* 58a).

3. When the person who presides over the assembly that is consecrating the new moon sings the praises of God, he does so in the presence of the *twelve* notable men of the town and *twelve chaverim* (companions) corresponding to the *twelve* tribes, the *twelve* months and the *twelve* constellations (various traditional sources).

THE NUMBER TWELVE IN JEWISH LIFE

The following are the appearances of the number twelve in Jewish life.

1. Twelve tribes of Israel (Reuben, Simeon, Levi, Judah, Issachar, Zebulun, Joseph, Benjamin, Dan, Naphtali, Gad, and Asher).
2. Twelve stones in the breastplate of the High Priest.
3. Twelve minor prophets (Hosea, Joel, Amos, Obadiah, Jonah, Micah, Nachum, Habakkuk, Zephaniah, Haggai, Zechariah, and Malachi).
4. Twelve months in the year.
5. Twelve constellations.

6. A Jewish girl is obligated to fulfill mitzvot at age twelve.
7. Twelve loaves of shewbread used in the Tabernacle.
8. Twelve portions in the Book of Genesis.
9. King Solomon became king at age twelve.

THE NUMBER THIRTEEN

THE NUMBER THIRTEEN IN THE BIBLE

The number thirteen plays a small role in biblical literature and a much more prominent one in rabbinic literature. Here is a sampling of the number thirteen in the Bible.

1. Age of Ishmael when circumcised (Genesis 17:25): "Ishmael was *thirteen* years of age when he was circumcised in the flesh of the foreskin."

2. Sacrificial offerings (Numbers 29:13): "You shall present a burnt offering, an offering by fire of pleasing odor to God: *thirteen* bulls of the herd, two rams . . ."

3. Number of years to build Solomon's palace (1 Kings 7:1): "It took Solomon *thirteen* years to build his palace, until his whole palace was completed."

4. Measurements of the Temple gate (Ezekiel 40:11): "He measured the opening of the gate and found it ten cubits wide, while the gate itself measured *thirteen* cubits across."

5. Thirteen Attributes of God (Exodus 34:6): "The Lord passed before him and proclaimed: 'The Lord, the

Lord, a God compassionate and gracious, slow to anger, abounding in kindness and faithfulness, extending kindness to the thousandth generation, forgiving iniquity, transgression and sin.' ''

THE NUMBER THIRTEEN
IN RABBINIC THOUGHT

The number thirteen does appear in rabbinic thought, often as a latent number. Here are several examples of the number thirteen in the rabbinic writings.

Thirteen Principles of Faith by Maimonides

1. "I believe with perfect faith that the Creator, blessed be Your Name, is the Author and Guide of everything that has been created and that God alone has made, does make, and will make all things.

2. "I believe . . . that the Creator, blessed be Your Name, is a Unity, and that there is no unity in any manner like You, and that You alone are our God, who was, is, and will be.

3. "I believe . . . that the Creator, blessed be Your Name, is not a body, and that You are free from all the accidents of matter, and that You have not any form whatsoever.

4. "I believe . . . that the Creator, blessed be Your Name, is the first and the last.

5. "I believe with perfect faith that to the Creator, blessed be Your Name, and to You alone, it is right to pray, and that it is not right to pray to any being besides You."

6. "I believe with perfect faith that all the words of the prophets are true.

7. "I believe with perfect faith that the prophecy of Moses our teacher was true and that he was the chief of the prophets, both of those that preceded and of those that followed him.

8. "I believe . . . that the whole Torah, now in our possession, is the same that was given to Moses our teacher.

9. "I believe . . . that this Torah will not be changed and that there will never be any other law from the Creator, blessed be Your Name.

10. "I believe . . . that the Creator, blessed be Your Name, knows every deed of the human race and all of their thoughts, as it is said, 'It is You who fashions the hearts of them all, that give heed to all their deeds.' "

11. "I believe . . . that the Creator, blessed be Your Name, rewards those that keep Your mitzvot and punishes those that transgress them.

12. "I believe . . . in the coming of the Messiah, and though the Messiah may tarry, I will wait daily for the coming of the Messiah.

13. "I believe . . . that there will be a resurrection of the dead at the time when it shall please the Creator, blessed be Your Name, and exalted be the remembrance of You forever and forever" (Maimonides, *Commentary on the Mishnah*).

Rabbi Ishmael's Thirteen Principles of Logic

1. "Inference from minor to major, and from major to minor.

2. "Inference from similarity of phrases in texts.

3. "A comprehensive principle derived from one text or from two related texts.

4. "A general proposition followed by a specifying particular.

5. "A particular term followed by a general proposition.

6. "A general law limited by a specific application and then treated again in general terms must be interpreted according to the tenor of the specific limitation.

7. "A general proposition requiring a particular or specific term to explain it, and conversely, a particular term requiring a general one to complement it.

8. "When a subject included in a general proposition is afterward particularly excepted to give information concerning it, the exception is made not for that one instance only but to apply to the general proposition as a whole.

9. "Whenever anything is first included in a general proposition and is then excepted to prove another similar proposition, this specifying alleviates and does not aggravate the law's restriction.

10. "But when anything is first included in a general proposition and is then excepted to state a case that is not a similar proposition, such specifying alleviates in some respects and in others aggravates the law's restriction.

11. "Anything included in a general proposition and afterward excepted to determine a new matter cannot be applied to the general proposition unless this be expressly done in the text.

12. "An interpretation may be deduced from the text or from subsequent terms of the text.

13. "In like manner, when two texts contradict each other, we follow the second, until a third text is found that reconciles the contradiction" (*Sifra,* ch. 1).

Mitzvot

"At *thirteen,* one is ready for mitzvot" (*Ethics of the Fathers* 5:13).

Eating Bread in the Morning

Thirteen things were said concerning eating bread in the morning:

It protects against heat and cold, winds and demons.
It makes the simple wise, causes a person to win lawsuits, and helps a person to study and teach Torah, to have his words heeded, and to retain scholarship.
A person who eats in the morning does not exhale a bad odor and lives with his wife without lusting after other women.
Morning bread also kills the worms in a person's intestines. And some people say it gets rid of jealousy and encourages love.
A proverb says: "Sixty runners speed along but cannot overtake the person who breaks bread in the morning."
(Talmud *Bava Metziah* 107b)

THE NUMBER FIFTEEN

THE NUMBER FIFTEEN IN JEWISH LIFE

Although the number fifteen is not prominent in biblical or rabbinical literature, it does play a latent role in Jewish life. Here are several number fifteens in Jewish life:

1. The letters of a Name of God, *yud-hey,* equal the number fifteen.
2. There were fifteen generations from Abraham to King Solomon.
3. There were fifteen types of materials contributed by the Israelites to the building of the sanctuary.
4. There were fifteen steps from the forecourt to the inner court of the Temple in Jerusalem.
5. King David wrote fifteen "Songs of Ascent," *shiray ma-alot.*
6. There are fifteen steps in the Passover seder service.

THE NUMBER TWENTY-FOUR

THE NUMBER TWENTY-FOUR IN THE BIBLE

Twenty-four plays a minor role in the Bible. Here are several verses in which it appears.

Sacrificial offerings (Numbers 7:88): "Total of herd offerings for sacrifices of well-being, *twenty-four* bulls."

Parts of the body (2 Samuel 21:20): "Once again there was fighting at Gath. There was a giant of a man, who had six fingers on each hand and six toes on each foot, *twenty-four* in all."

Rule of the king (1 Kings 16:33): "In the third year of King Asa of Judah, Baasha son of Ahijah became king in Tirzah over all Israel—for *twenty-four* years."

THE NUMBER TWENTY-FOUR
IN RABBINIC THOUGHT

The following are some sample selections of the number twenty-four as it appears in rabbinic thought.

Twenty-four things hinder repentance:

1. "The person who leads the people to sin.
2. "One who diverts another from the good to the evil.

3. "One who sees that his son is falling into bad ways and does not stop him.
4. "One who says, 'I will sin and then repent.'
5. "One who stands aloof from the community.
6. "One who opposes the rulings of the sages. . . .
7. "One who makes a mockery of Divine precepts.
8. "One who insults his teachers.
9. "One who hates rebuke.
10. "One who curses the people and not an individual, of whom he might ask to forgive him.
11. "One who shares with a thief.
12. "One who finds lost property and does not announce it.
13. "One who despoils the poor, orphans, or widows.
14. "One who takes bribes to tamper with justice.
15. "One who shares a meal that is insufficient for its owner.
16. "One who makes use of a poor man's pledge.
17. "One who gazes lustfully at women.
18. "One who elevates himself at the expense of another's degradation.
19. "One who suspects honest men and says to himself that it is no sin.
20. "Gossip.
21. "Slander.
22. "Wrath.
23. "Evil thought.
24. "Keeping bad company." (Maimonides, *Mishneh Torah,* Laws of Repentance)

"Learning in the Torah is greater than priesthood or kingship, for kingship is acquired by thirty qualifications, priesthood by *twenty-four*" (*Ethics of the Fathers* 6:6).

THE NUMBER THIRTY-NINE

THE NUMBER THIRTY-NINE IN THE BIBLE

The number thirty-nine is most noteworthy for the thirty-nine categories of forbidden work as enumerated in the Talmud (Talmud *Shabbat* 7:2). Here is a summary of the thirty-nine prohibited activities, which represent a cross-section of all of the main types of human productivity. All of these activities relate to acts that show a person's mastery over the world by the constructive exercise of one's intelligence and skill.

1. Plowing
2. Sowing
3. Reaping
4. Sheaf making
5. Threshing
6. Winnowing
7. Selecting
8. Sifting
9. Grinding
10. Kneading
11. Baking

12. Sheep shearing
13. Bleaching
14. Combing raw materials
15. Dyeing
16. Spinning
17–19: Weaving operations
20. Separating into threads
21. Tying a knot
22. Untying a knot
23. Sewing
24. Tearing
25. Trapping or hunting
26. Slaughtering
27. Skinning
28. Tanning
29. Scraping pelts
30. Marking out
31. Cutting to shape
32. Writing
33. Erasing
34. Building
35. Demolishing
36. Kindling a fire
37. Extinguishing
38. The final hammer blow
39. Carrying from private to public or vice versa

THE NUMBER FORTY

THE NUMBER FORTY IN THE BIBLE

Forty is an important round number, indicating a relatively long period of time. The length of a generation, for example, is approximately forty years. The following is a listing of examples of the appearance of the number forty in the Bible.

1. The span of human life is three times forty years (Genesis 6:3): "God said, 'My breath shall not abide in man forever, since he, too, is flesh; let the days allowed him be *one hundred and twenty* years.'"

2. Years to attain full adulthood (Joshua 14:7): "[Caleb said:] I was *forty* years old when Moses the servant of the Lord sent me from Kadesh Barnea to spy out the land, and I gave him a forthright report."

3. The time span representing old age is two times forty years (2 Samuel 19:33): "Barzillai was very old, *eighty* years of age. And he had provided the king with food during his stay at Machanaim."

4. Years of Israelite wanderings in the wilderness (Exodus 16:35): "And the Israelites ate manna for *forty* years, until they came to a settled land."

5. Years for which the land of Israel had rest (Judges 3:11): "He prevailed over Cushan-rishathaim, and the land had rest [i.e., peace] for *forty* years."

6. Total number of years of various reigns of kings:

King David (2 Samuel 5:4): "King David was thirty years old when he became king, and he reigned for *forty* years."
King Solomon (1 Kings 11:42): "The length of Solomon's reign in Jerusalem, over all Israel, was *forty* years."
King Jehoash (2 Chronicles 24:1): "Jehoash was seven years old when he became king, and he reigned in Jerusalem for *forty* years."

7. Days of the deluge in the time of Noah (Genesis 7:4): "For in seven days time I will make it rain upon the earth, *forty* days and *forty* nights, and I will blot out from the earth all existence that I created."

8. Days for which Moses remained on the top of Mount Sinai (Exodus 24:18): "Moses went inside the cloud and ascended the mountain, and Moses remained on the mountain *forty* days and *forty* nights."

9. Days of scouting of the spies (Numbers 13:25): "At the end of *forty* days, they [the spies] returned from scouting the land."

10. Days of the stand of Goliath (1 Samuel 17:16): "The Philistine stepped forward morning and evening and took his stand for *forty* days."

11. Numbers of days until doomsday for the people of Nineveh (Jonah 3:4): "Jonah started out and made his way into the city the distance of one day's walk, and proclaimed: '*Forty* days more, and Nineveh shall be overthrown.' "

12. Number of lashes for breaking the law (Deuteronomy 25:3): "He may be given up to *forty* lashes."

13. Temple measurements (Ezekiel 41:2): "Next he measured the depth of the hall, *forty* cubits."

14. Forty thousand, indicating a very large number (Joshua 4:13): "About *forty thousand* shock troops went across, at the instance of God, to the steppes of Jericho for battle."

THE NUMBER FORTY IN RABBINIC THOUGHT

Here are several examples of the number forty as it appears in rabbinic writings.

1. "Food is better for a man up to age *forty.* After *forty,* drink is better" (Talmud *Shabbat* 152).

2. "Rabbah, who merely studied Torah, lived *forty* years. Abbaye, who studied the Torah and also practiced benevolence, lived sixty" (Talmud *Rosh Hashanah* 18a).

3. "Moses spent *forty* years in Pharaoh's palace, *forty* years in Midian, and *forty* as a leader of Israel" (*Midrash Bereshit Rabbah* 100:11).

4. "Hillel the Elder ascended from Babylon to Israel at the age of *forty,* studied under his teachers for *forty* years, and led Israel for *forty* years" (various traditional sources).

5. "Rabbi Akiba shepherded flocks for *forty* years, studied Torah for *forty* years, and taught Israel for *forty* years" (*Sifre,* Deuteronomy 34:7).

6. In exceptional cases, outstanding righteous persons undertook to fast for long periods, eating only at night. Rabbi Tzaddok fasted in this manner for *forty*

years in an attempt to avert the destruction of the Holy Temple (Talmud *Gittin* 56a).

7. "Rabbi Yosef fasted *forty* years so that his descendants would never forget the Torah" (Talmud *Bava Metziah* 88a).

8. "At *forty* years of age, one attains insight" (*Ethics of the Fathers* 5:21).

9. "A man does not comprehend his teacher's full intention and the wisdom of his teaching until after *forty* years" (Talmud *Avodah Zarah* 5b).

10. "Neither the study of Kabbalah [mysticism] nor a judgment in decisive legal problems should be undertaken before one reaches the age of *forty*" (*Code of Jewish Law, Yoreh Deah* 246:4).

11. "There were *forty* generations from Moses, who was taught the Torah in *forty* days until Rabbi Ashi, who compiled the Oral Law in the Babylonian Talmud" (*Rambam LeMishnah,* intro.).

12. "Resh Lakish repeated his studies *forty* times, corresponding to the *forty* days that Moses spent atop Mount Sinai to acquire the Torah" (Talmud *Taanit* 8a).

13. "Rabbi Eliezer said: The days of the Messiah will last *forty* years, as it is written, '*Forty* years long shall I take hold of the generation [Psalm 95:10].' " (Talmud *Sanhedrin* 99a).

THE NUMBER FORTY-EIGHT

THE NUMBER FORTY-EIGHT IN THE BIBLE

The number forty-eight plays a minor role in biblical numerology. It is mentioned in reference to Levitical cities (Numbers 35:7): "Thus the total number of the towns that you assign to the Levites shall be *forty-eight* towns, with their pasture."

THE NUMBER FORTY-EIGHT
IN RABBINIC THOUGHT

The following is an example of the number forty-eight as it appears in rabbinic thought.

"Learning in the Torah is greater than the priesthood or kingship, for kingship is acquired by thirty qualifications, priesthood by twenty-four, but learning in the Torah by *forty-eight*. And they are: by study, by attentive listening, by distinct speech, by understanding of the heart, by awe, by reverence, by humility, by cheerfulness, by purity, by attendance on the sages, by associating with fellow students, by close argument with disciples, by sedateness, by knowledge of Scripture and Mishnah, by moderation in business, worldly occupation, pleasure, sleep, conversation, and jesting, by long-suffering, by a good heart, by faith in the sages, by submission to sorrows, by recognizing one's place, by rejoicing in one's lot, by making a fence around one's words, by claiming no merit for oneself, by being beloved, by loving the All Present, by loving humankind, by loving well-doing, by loving rectitude and reproof, by shunning honor and not boasting of one's learning, and not delighting in making decisions, who helps his fellow to bear his yoke, and who judges him favorably, directing him to truth and peace; and who is composed in one's study; by asking and answering, hearing and adding to it; who learns in order to teach and who learns in order to practice; by making one's master wiser, and retells exactly what he has heard, and reports a thing in the name of him who said it." (*Ethics of the Fathers* 6:6)

THE NUMBER FIFTY

THE NUMBER FIFTY IN THE BIBLE

The number fifty, which is a multiple of ten, occurs with frequency in the Bible, usually in reference to weights, measurements, and compensation. Here is a sampling of mentions of the number fifty in the Bible.

1. Measurement of Noah's ark (Genesis 6:15:): "This is how you shall make it: the length of the ark shall be three hundred cubits, its width *fifty* cubits."

2. Temple measurements (Ezekiel 40:15): "And the distance from the front of the outer gate to the front of the inner vestibule of the gate was *fifty* cubits."

3. Countdown to the festival of Shavuot (Leviticus 23:16): "You must count until the day after the seventh week, *fifty* days, then you shall bring an offering of new grain to God."

4. Payment to the father of a woman who is seized and raped (Deuteronomy 23:28): "If a man comes upon a virgin who is not engaged and he seizes her and lies with her, and they are discovered, the man who lay

with her shall pay the girl's father *fifty* shekels of silver, and she shall be his wife.''

5. Five hundred (fifty times ten), representing a very large number (Genesis 5:32): "When Noah had lived *five hundred* years, he begot Shem, Ham, and Japheth.''

THE NUMBER FIFTY IN RABBINIC THOUGHT

Here is a selection in which the number fifty appears in rabbinic thought.

1. "Poverty is more grievous than *fifty* plagues" (*Bava Batra* 116).

2. "*Fifty* [is the age] for giving advice" (*Ethics of the Fathers* 5:21).

THE NUMBER SIXTY

THE NUMBER SIXTY IN THE BIBLE

The number sixty, which is the basis of the sexagesimal system, is purportedly said to be a legacy from the Sumerians, whose methodology of calculation has left its mark on civilization. The division of the circle into 360 degrees, of an hour into 60 minutes, and a minute into 60 seconds, and counting using the units of the dozen and the gross (i.e., twelve dozen) is derived from the Sumerians. The following are some biblical sources of the number sixty.

1. Persons' ages (Genesis 5:15): "Mechalel lived to be *sixty* years of age."

2. Vowing and valuation of a person (Leviticus 27:22): "When anyone explicitly vows to God the equivalent for a human being, the following scale shall apply: If it is a male from twenty to *sixty* years of age, the equivalent is fifty shekels of silver by sanctuary weight."

THE NUMBER SIXTY IN RABBINIC THOUGHT

Here are some selections in which the number sixty appears.

1. "Rabbah, who merely studied the Torah, lived forty years. Abbaye, who studied the Torah and also practiced benevolence, lived *sixty*" (Talmud *Rosh Hashanah* 18a).

2. "Rabbah said: Life, sons, and wealth do not depend upon merit but upon bad luck. Rabbah and Rabbi Chisda were both righteous rabbis. When either prayed for rain, it came. Yet, Rabbi Chisda lived for ninety-two years and Rabbah only for forty; in the house of Rabbi Chisda there were *sixty* weddings, in the house of Rabbah *sixty* deaths" (*Mechilta* 28a).

3. "A man once said, When our love was strong, we could sleep on a bed no wider than a sword's edge; now that our love is not strong, a bed of *sixty* cells is too small for us" (*Genesis Rabbah, Vayishlach* 75:4).

4. "*Sixty* for old age . . ." (*Ethics of the Fathers* 5:21).

THE NUMBER SEVENTY

THE NUMBER SEVENTY IN THE BIBLE

The number seventy (i.e., the product of two sacred numbers, seven times ten) is generally used as a round figure, with some sacred allusions. It occurs in a number of different contexts of the Bible.

1. Years of Kenan's life when he finally had a child (Genesis 5:12): "When Kenan had lived *seventy* years, he begot Mechalel."

2. Number of elders of Israel (Exodus 24:1): "Then God said to Moses, 'Come up to the Lord, with Aaron, Nadav and Avihu, and *seventy* elders of Israel' "

3. Offerings and their values (Exodus 38:29): "The copper from the elevation offering came to *seventy* talents, and two thousand, four hundred shekels."

4. Number of family members of Jacob who went down to Egypt (Exodus 1:5): "The total number of persons that were of Jacob's issue came to *seventy.*"

5. Number of years for which the nations will serve the Babylonian king (Jeremiah 25:11): "And those nations that will serve the king of Babylon *seventy* years."

THE NUMBER SEVENTY IN RABBINIC THOUGHT

1. Gog and Magog have the numerical value of *seventy,* namely, the *seventy* nations. (Note: Jewish tradition states that humankind is made up of seventy nations.)

2. "The Torah was transmitted to *seventy* elders" (*Midrash Yelamdeinu*).

3. "There are *seventy* facets to the Torah" (*Zohar Bereshit* 36).

4. "*Seventy* facets to the Torah were translated into *seventy* languages in order to make it understandable to the *seventy* nations" (Talmud *Sotah* 32a).

5. "On the Festival of Sukkot, *seventy* sacrifices were offered for the sake of the *seventy* nations of the world who have *seventy* representatives among the heavenly angels" (*Midrash Alpha Beita*).

6. "Rabbi Eleazar said: To what do the *seventy* bullocks that were offered during the seven days of Sukkot correspond? To the *seventy* nations of the earth" (Talmud *Sukkah* 55b).

THE NUMBER SEVENTY IN JEWISH LIFE

1. After the flood, *seventy* nations descended from Noah.

2. *Seventy* languages emerged at the building of the Tower of Babel.

3. The Jewish People began with the *seventy* people who came with Jacob to Egypt.

4. In the World to Come, *seventy* prime nations will recognize God as the One and Only God of the world (*Maharal, Gevurot*).

THE NUMBER ONE THOUSAND

THE NUMBER ONE THOUSAND IN THE BIBLE

The number one thousand and its many multiples occur with frequency in the Bible as round numbers indicating a large quantity. It has been said that the Hebrew word for one thousand, *elef,* denotes "a crowd," and at times in the Bible it has the sense of a clan or military unit, without regard to number of persons in that unit. Multiples of one thousand are often used as hyperboles in the Bible. Here are some sample verses in which the number one thousand occurs.

1. An amount of money (Genesis 21:16): "And Avimelech said to Hagar, 'I herewith give your brother *one thousand* pieces of silver; this will serve you as vindication before all who are with you, and you are cleared before everyone.' "

2. Number of Israelites sent to battle the Midianites (Numbers 31:4): "You shall dispatch on the campaign *one thousand* from every one of the tribes of Israel."

3. Number of deaths at the Tower of Schechem (Judges 9:49): "Thus all the people of the Tower of Schechem also perished, about *one thousand* men and women."

4. Animal sacrifices: (1 Chronicles 29:221): "They offered sacrifices to God and made burnt offerings to God on the morrow of that day: *one thousand* bulls, *one thousand* rams, *one thousand* lambs, with their libations."

5. Number one thousand representing a military unit (Exodus 18:21): "You shall also seek out from among all the people capable men who fear God, trustworthy men who spurn ill-gotten gain. Set these over them as chiefs of *thousands,* hundreds, fifties, and tens."

6. The following are samples of multiples of one thousand used in the Bible as hyperbole:

i. "Five of you shall give chase to one hundred, and a hundred of you shall give chase to *ten thousand*" (Leviticus 26:8).

ii. "God sent a pestilence upon Israel from morning until the set time, and *seventy thousand* of the people died, from Dan to Beersheba" (2 Samuel 24:15).

iii. "A river of fire streamed forth before Him. *Thousands* upon *thousands* served Him; *myriads* upon *myriads* (i.e., *one million*) attended Him" (Daniel 7:10).

ONE THOUSAND IN RABBINIC THOUGHT

Here are two samples of the number one thousand and its various multiples as they appear in rabbinic writings.

1. "Rabbi was preaching and the audience seemed to lose interest. Suddenly he said: 'A woman in Egypt gave birth to 600,000.' 'Who was this?' they asked. 'Jochebed,' he answered, 'for she gave birth to Moses, the

equal of all Israel, as it is written: "Then sang Moses and Israel" ' " (*Midrash Song of Songs* 1).

2. " 'The Lord talked with you face to face in the mount [Deuteronomy 5:4]' Rabbi Jochanan said: A *thousand* people look at a statue, and each one says, "It is at me that the statue is looking." So God looks at every single Israelite, and says, "I am the Lord your God." Rabbi Levi said: You can learn the same lesson from everyday life. One voice can enter ten ears, but ten voices cannot enter one ear. Yet God hears the prayers of all His creatures as if they were one prayer, as it says, 'O Thou that hears prayers' " (*Pesikta Rabbati* 100b).

SOME FASCINATING NUMBERS IN JEWISH LIFE

The following are some interesting Jewish numerical lists culled from various sources.

BIBLE AND PROPHETIC PORTIONS BY THE NUMBERS

On every Sabbath and Jewish holiday, one or more portions are recited from the Torah. In general, the Sabbaths are named according to the main portion. Here are the numbers that one needs to know, as they relate to the weekly Torah portions as well as the prophetic readings. The first number that appears next to each portion is the chapter in the Bible where the portion is located. Numbers appearing after the colon refer to the verses in that chapter.

Name		Torah Text	Prophetic Reading
Bereishit	Genesis	1:1-6:8	Isaiah 42:5-43:11 (42:5-21)
Noach		6:9-11:32	Isaiah 54:1-55:5 (54:1-10)

Lech Lecha	12:1-17:27	Isaiah 40:27-41:16
Vayera	18:1-22:24	2 Kings 4:1-37 (4:1-23)
Chaye Sarah	23:1-25:18	1 Kings 1:1-31.
Toledot	25:19-28:9	Malachi 1:1-2:7
Vayetzei	28:10-32:3	Hosea 12:12-14:10 (11:17-12:12)
Vayishlach	32:4-36:43	Hosea 11:17-12:12 (Obadiah 1:1-21)
Vayeshev	37:1-40:23	Amos 2:6-3:8
Mikketz	41:1-44:17	1 Kings 3:15-4:1
Vayigash	44:18-47:27	Ezekiel 37:15-25
Vayechi	47:28-50:26	1 Kings 2:1-12
Shemot Exodus	1:1-6:1	Isaiah 27:6-28:13; 29:22-23 (Jeremiah 1:1-2:3)
Vaeyra	6:2-9:35	Ezekiel 28:25-29:21
Bo	10:1-13:16	Jeremiah 46:13-28
Beshallach	13:17-17:16	Judges 4:4-5:31 (5:1-31)
Yitro	18:1-20:23	Isaiah 6:1-7:6; 9:5-6 (6:1-13)
Mishpatim	21:1-24:18	Jeremiah 34:8-22; 33:25-26
Terumah	25:1-27:19	1 Kings 5:26-6:13
Tetzaveh	27:20-30:10	Ezekiel 43:10-27

Ki Tisa	30:11-34:35	1 Kings 18:1-39 (18:20-39)
Vayakhel	35:1-38:20	1 Kings 7:40-50 (7:13-26)
Pekudei	38:21-40:38	1 Kings 7:51-8:21 (7:40-50)
Vayikra Leviticus	1:1-5:26	Isaiah 43:21-44:23
Tzav	6:1-8:36	Jeremiah 7:21-8:3; 9:22-23
Shemini	9:1-11:47	2 Samuel 6:1-7:17 (6:1-19)
Tazria	12:1-13:59	2 Kings 4:42-5:19
Metzora	14:1-15:33	2 Kings 7:3-20
Acharei Mot	16:1-18:30	Ezekiel 22:1-19 (22:1-16)
Kedoshim	19:1-20:27	Amos 9:7-15 (Ezekiel 20:2-20)
Emor	21:1-24:23	Ezekiel 44:15-31
Behar	25:1-26:2	Jeremiah 32:6-27
Bechukotai	26:3-27:34	Jeremiah 16:19-17:14
Bemidar Numbers	1:1-4:20	Hosea 2:1-22
Naso	4:21-7:89	Judges 13:2-25
Behaalotecha	8:1-12:16	Zechariah 2:14-4:7
Shelach	13:1-15:41	Joshua 2:1-24
Korach	16:1-18:32	1 Samuel 11:14-12:22
Chukat	19:1-22:1	Judges 11:1-33
Balak	22:2-25:9	Micah 5:6-6:8

Pinchas		25:10-30:1	1 Kings 18:46-19:21
Mattot		30:2-32:42	Jeremiah 1:1-2:3
Masey		33:1-36:13	Jeremiah 2:4-28; 3:4 (2:4-28; 4:1-2)
Devarim	Deuteronomy	1:1-3:22	Isaiah 1:1-27
Va-etchanan		3:23-7:11	Isaiah 40:1-26
Ekev		7:12-11:25	Isaiah 49:14-51:3
Re'eh		11:26-16:17	Isaiah 54:11-55:5
Shofetim		16:18-21:9	Isaiah 51:12-52:12
Ki Tetze		21:10-25:19	Isaiah 54:1-10
Ki Tavo		26:1-29:8	Isaiah 60:1-22
Nitzavim		29:9-30:20	Isaiah 61:10-63:9
Vayelech		31:1-30	Isaiah 55:6-56:8
Haazinu		32:1-52	2 Samuel 22:1-51
Vezot Ha-berachah		33:1-34:12	Joshua 1:1-18 (1:1-9)

Note: parentheses indicate Sephardic ritual

Special Readings

Rosh Hashanah	1st Day	Genesis 21:1-34; Numbers 29:1-6	1 Samuel 1:1-2:10
	2nd Day	Genesis 22:1-24; Numbers 29:1-6	Jeremiah 31:2-20
Shabbat Shuvah		Weekly portion	Hosea 14:2-10; Micah 7:18-20 or Hosea 14:2-10; (Hosea 14:2-10; Micah 7:18-20)
Yom Kippur	Morning	Leviticus 16:1-34; Numbers 29:7-11	Isaiah 57:14-58:14

Sukkot	1st Day	Leviticus 22:26-23:44; Numbers 29:12-16	Zechariah 14:1-21
	2nd Day	Leviticus 22:26-23:44; Numbers 29:12-16	1 Kings 8:2-21
Shabbat Chol Hamoed	Sukkot	Exodus 33:12-34:26; Daily portion from Numbers 29	Ezekiel 38:18-39:16
	8th Day	Deuteronomy 14:22-16:17; Numbers 29:35-30:1	1 Kings 8:56-66
Simchat Torah		Deuteronomy 33:1-34:12; Genesis 1:1-2:3 Numbers 29:35-30:1	Joshua 1:1-18 (1:1-9)
1st Shabbat Chanukah		Weekly and Chanukah portions	Zechariah 2:14-4:7
2nd Shabbat Chanukah		Weekly and Chanukah portions	1 Kings 7:40-50
Shabbat Shekalim		Weekly portion; Exodus 30:11-16	2 Kings 12:1-17 (11:17-12:17)
Shabbat Zachor		Weekly portion; Deuteronomy 25:17-19	2 Samuel 15:2-34 (15:1-34)

Shabbat Parah		Weekly portion:	Ezekiel 36:16-38
		Numbers 19:1-22	(36:16-36)
Shabbat Hachodesh		Weekly portion:	Ezekiel 45:16-46:18
		Exodus 12:1-20	(45:18-46:15)
Shabbat Hagadol		Weekly portion	Malachi 3:4-24
Pesach	1st Day	Exodus 12:21-51;	Joshua 3:5-7; 5:2-6:1;
		Numbers 28:16-25	6:27 (5:2-6:1)
	2nd Day	Leviticus 22:26-23:44;	2 Kings 23:1-9; 21-25
		Numbers 28:16-25	
Shabbat Pesach		Exodus 33:12-34:26;	Ezekiel 36:37-37:14
		Numbers 28:19-25	(37:1-14)
	7th Day	Exodus 13:17-15:26;	2 Samuel 22:1-51
		Numbers 28:19-25	
	8th Day	Deuteronomy 15:19-16:17; (on Shabbat 14:22-16:17)	Isaiah 10:32-12:6
		Numbers 28:19-25	
Shavuot	1st Day	Exodus 19:11-23	Ezekiel 1:1-28;3:12
		Numbers 28:26-31	

	2nd Day	Deuteronomy 15:19-16:17	Habakkuk 3:1-19
		(on Shabbat 14:22-6:17)	(2:20-3:19)
		Numbers 28:26-31	
Tisha B'av	Morning	Deuteronomy 4:25-40	Jeremiah 8:13-9:23
	Afternoon	Exodus 32:11-14 34:1-10	Isaiah 55:6-56:8
Shabbat Rosh Chodesh		Weekly portion	Isaiah 66:1-24
Shabbat immediately preceding Rosh Chodesh	Weekly portion	1 Samuel 20:18-42	

JEWISH CITY NUMEROLOGY

Estimated Jewish Population of Some Foreign Cities

Amsterdam	15,000
Antwerp	15,000
Brussels	23,000
Buenos Aires	220,000
Copenhagen	6,700
Glasgow	11,000
Istanbul	22,000
Johannesburg	63,620
Kiev	152,000
Leningrad	165,000

London	225,000
Marseilles	70,000
Melbourne	40,000
Milan	10,000
Montreal	100,000
Moscow	250,000
Nice	25,000
Odessa	120,000
Ottawa	9,000
Paris	350,000
Rio de Janeiro	29,000
Rome	15,000
Stockholm	8,000
Sydney	33,000
Toronto	120,000
Vancouver	18,000
Winnepeg	16,000
Zurich	6,713

Estimated Jewish Population of Cities and Counties in the United States

Alabama

Birmingham	5,100
Montgomery	1,300

Alaska

Anchorage	2,000

Arizona

Phoenix	50,000
Tucson	20,000

Arkansas
Little Rock	1,300

California
Alameda and Contra Costa Counties	51,500
Fresno	2,000
Long Beach	13,500
Los Angeles Metro Area	501,000
Orange County	80,000
Sacramento	12,500
San Diego	70,000
San Francisco Bay Area	210,000
Santa Monica	8,000
Ventura County	9,000

Colorado
Colorado Springs	1,500
Denver	46,000

Connecticut
Bridgeport	18,000
Hartford	28,000
New Haven	28,000
Norwalk	9,500
Stamford	11,100
Waterbury	2,700

Delaware
Dover	650
Wilmington	9,500

District of Columbia
Greater Washington	165,000

Florida
Boca Raton-Delray	52,000
Fort Lauderdale	140,000
Hollywood	66,000
Jacksonville	7,300
Miami and Dade Counties	226,000
Orlando	18,000
Palm Beach County (except Boca Raton)	55,000
Sarasota	9,500
St. Petersburg	9,500
Tampa	12,500

Georgia
Atlanta Metro Area	67,000
Augusta	1,400
Savannah	2,750

Hawaii
Honolulu (includes all of Oahu)	6,400

Idaho
Boise	220

Illinois
Champaign—Urbana	1,300
Chicago Metro Area	248,000
Rockford	1,000
Springfield	1,000

Indiana
Bloomington	1,000
Ft. Wayne	1,085

Gary	2,200
Indianapolis	10,000
South Bend	1,900
Iowa	
Des Moines	2,800
Iowa City	1,200
Kansas	
Topeka	500
Wichita	1,000
Kentucky	
Lexington	2,000
Louisville	8,700
Louisiana	
Baton Rouge	1,200
New Orleans	12,000
Shreveport	960
Maine	
Augusta	500
Bangor	1,250
Portland	3,900
Maryland	
Annapolis	2,000
Baltimore	94,500
Hartford County	1,000
Howard County	7,200
Massachusetts	
Andover	3,000
Boston Metro Region	228,000

Cape Cod	3,000
Fall River	1,780
Greenfield	900
Haverhill	1,500
Lawrence	2,250
Lowell	2,000
Lynn-North Shore Area	25,000
New Bedford	3,000
Pittsfield	3,100
Springfield	11,000
Taunton	1,200
Worchester County	13,700

Michigan

Ann Arbor	5,000
Detroit Metro Area	94,000
Flint	2,000
Grand Rapids	1,725
Kalamazoo	1,000
Lansing	2,100

Minnesota

Duluth	500
Minneapolis	22,000
St. Paul	7,500

Mississippi

Greenville	270
Jackson	700

Missouri

Kansas City Metro Area	19,100
St. Louis	53,500

Montana

Billings   200

Nebraska

Lincoln   1,000
Omaha   6,500

Nevada

Las Vegas   19,000
Reno   1,400

New Hampshire

Manchester   2,500
Portsmouth   950

New Jersey

Atlantic City   15,800
Bergen County   85,000
Camden and   28,000
Cherry Hill
Essex County   76,200
Flemington   900
Jersey City   5,500
Middlesex County   58,000
Monmouth County   33,600
Morris-Sussex Counties   33,500
Ocean County   9,500
Passaic County-Clifton   18,700
Princeton   3,00
Somerset County   7,900
Union County   30,000
Vineland   2,200

New Mexico
Albuquerque	4,000
Sante Fe	900

New York
Albany	12,000
Binghamton	3,000
Buffalo	18,125
Ellenville	1,600
Ithaca	1,250
Kingston	4,300
Liberty	2,100
Monticello	2,400
New York Metro Area	1,450,000
Orange County	10,000
Poughkeepsie	6,500
Rochester	22,500
Rockland County	83,100
Schenectady	5,200
Sullivan County	7,425
Syracuse	9,000
Utica	1,900

North Carolina
Asheville	1,350
Chapel Hill-Durham	3,000
Charlotte	4,000
Greensboro	2,700
Raleigh	3,000

North Dakota
Fargo	500

Ohio

Akron	6,000
Butler County	900
Canton	2,400
Cincinnati	23,000
Cleveland	65,000
Columbus	15,600
Dayton	6,000
Toledo	6,300
Youngstown	4,000

Oklahoma

Oklahoma City	2,500
Tulsa	2,750

Oregon

Eugene	2,300
Portland	12,000

Pennsylvania

Allentown	6,000
Chester County	4,000
Easton	1,200
Harrisburg	6,500
Lancaster	2,100
Lower Bucks County	14,500
Philadelphia Area	250,000
Pittsburgh	45,000
Reading	2,800
Scranton	3,150
Wilkes-Barre	3,200
York	1,500

Rhode Island

Providence	14,200
Washington County	1,200

South Carolina

Charleston	4,000
Columbia	2,000
Greenville	800

South Dakota

Sioux Falls	135

Tennessee

Chattanooga	1,350
Knoxville	1,350
Memphis	8,800
Nashville	5,600

Texas

Austin	5,000
Beaumont	800
Corpus Christi	1,400
Dallas	35,000
El Paso	4,900
Ft. Worth	5,000
Houston	42,000
San Antonio	10,000

Utah

Salt Lake City	2,800

Vermont

Burlington	3,000
Newport	550

Virginia

Charlottesville	950
Newport News	2,000
Norfolk-Virginia Beach	18,000
Portsmouth	1,900
Richmond	8,000
Roanoke	1,050

Washington

Seattle	29,300
Spokane	800
Tacoma	1,100

West Virginia

Charleston	1,000

Wisconsin

Madison	4,500
Milwaukee	28,000

Wyoming

Cheyenne	230
United States total	5,798,000

NUMEROLOGY
AND THE JEWISH CALENDAR

The Jewish calendar is so formulated that the first day of Passover never falls on a Monday, Wednesday, or Friday. The first six days of Passover always will determine the days of the week when the other Festivals will occur. This has been fixed by an ingenious device of combining the first six letters of the Hebrew alphabet with the last six, in reverse order. For example, the first letter is joined with the last letter, the second letter with the next-to-the-last letter, and so forth. This results in these combinations.

א,,,,ת,ב,,,,ש,ג,,,,ר,ד,,,,ק,ה,,,,צ,ו,,,,ף

The days of Passover will always fall as follows:

א	First day on Tishah be-Av	תשעה באב
ב	Second day on Shavuot	שבועות
ג	Third day on Rosh ha-Shanah	ראש השנה
ד	Fourth day on Simhat Torah	קריאת התורה שהיא שמחת תורה
ה	Fifth day on Yom Kippur	צום כפור
ו	Sixth day on the previous Purim	פורים

Recently, another combination, ז,,,,ע, consisting of the seventh letter of the alphabet, corresponding to the seventh day of Passover, and the seventh letter from the last, which denotes Independence Day of the State of Israel, has been added:

ז	Seventh day on Israel Independence Day	יוח עצמעות

JEWISH LEAP YEAR NUMEROLOGY

In a span of nineteen years there are seven leap years, in which a complete month, called Adar II, is added. The distribution of leap years in a nineteen-year cycle is as follows: year 3, year 6, year 8, year 11, year 14, year 17, and year 19. If the number of the Hebrew year is divided by 19, the quotient indicates the number of cycles that have passed. The remainder indicates the kind of year: it is a leap year, if it is 3, 6, 11, 14, 17, or 19; otherwise, it is a common year.

For example, let us suppose that the year is 5713. To find out whether it is a leap year or a common year, we divide by 19. The quotient is 300 and the remainder is 13. Thus, the year 5713 is the 13th year in the 301st cycle, and therefore a common year.

BIBLE STATISTICS

The Bible has more than 773,000 words and 3.5 million letters. There are thirty-nine books in the Jewish Bible, 929 chapters, and 23,214 verses.

MASSORETIC NUMEROLOGY

The Massoretes were a group of scribes who cataloged and numbered the total number of verses, *sedrot* (weekly Bible portions), and chapters of each of the Five Books of Moses. Here is a summary of their findings.

Book of Genesis:
Total number of verses is 1,534
Total number of *sedrot* is 12
Total number of smaller divisions according
to the triennial cycle is 43
Total number of chapters is 50

Book of Exodus:
Total number of verses is 1,209
Total number of *sedrot* is 11
Total number of smaller divisions is 29
Total number of chapters is 40

Book of Leviticus:
Total number of verses is 859
Total number of *sedrot* is 10

Total number of smaller divisions is 23
Total number of chapters is 27

Book of Numbers:
Total number of verses is 1,288
Total number of *sedrot* is 10
Total number of smaller divisions is 32
Total number of chapters is 36

Book of Deuteronomy:
Total number of verses is 955
Total number of *sedrot* is 11
Total number of smaller divisions is 27
Total number of chapters is 34

Total number of verses in the Five Books of Moses is 5,845

NUMBER OF TIMES CERTAIN NAMES ARE MENTIONED IN THE FIVE BOOKS OF MOSES

Moses, 662
Children of Israel, 364
Aaron, 301
Pharaoh, 210
Jacob, 202
Joseph, 173
Isaac, 98
Esau, 80
Bilaam, 55
Judah, 48
Reuben, 45
Rachel, 44
Levi, 41
Noah, 40
Balak, 40
Sarah, 38
Leah, 33

Gad, 33
Lot, 32
Benjamin, 31
Rebekkah, 30
Joshua, 28
Ephraim, 26
Dan, 26
Simeon, 25
Asher, 20
Issachar, 19
Zebulun, 19
Naftali, 19
Gershon, 19
Ishmael, 17

NUMBER OF TIMES EACH HEBREW LETTER IS MENTIONED IN THE FIVE BOOKS OF MOSES

Aleph, 42,377
Beit, 38,218
Gimel, 29,537
Dalet, 32,530
Hey, 47,754
Vov, 76,922
Zayin, 22,867
Chet, 23,447
Tet, 11,052
Yud, 66,420
Chaf, 37,272
Final *chaf,* 10,981
Lamed, 41,517
Mem, 52,805
Final *Mem,* 24,973
Nun, 32,977
Final *Nun,* 8,719

Samach, 13,580
Ayin, 20,175
Pey, 20,750
Final *Pey,* 1,975
Tzaddi, 16,950
Final *Tzaddi,* 4,872
Kuf, 22,972
Reish, 22,147
Shin, Sin, 32,148
Tav, 36,140

TEN TORAH PORTIONS
WITH THE MOST VERSES

Naso, 176
Pinchas, 164
Bamidbar, 159
Vayishlach, 154
Noah, 153
Vayetze, 148
Vayera, 147
Bereishit, 146
Mikketz, 146
Ki Tissa, 139

LONGEST VERSE IN THE BIBLE

The longest verse in the Bible appears in the Book of Esther (8:9), which has forty-three words in Hebrew.

RABBINIC *TANNAIM* (TEACHERS) MENTIONED
MOST TIMES IN THE MISHNAH

Rabbi Yehuda bar Iloyi, 607 times
Rabbi Yossi bar Chalafta, 335 times

Rabbi Shimon bar Yochai, 326 times
Rabbi Meir, 323 times
Rabbi Eliezer ben Hyrcanus, 303 times
Rabbi Akiba, 278 times
Hillel, 236 times
Shammai, 235 times
Rabbi Yehoshua bar Chanina, 147 times
Rabbi Shimon ben Gamliel, 101 times

AGES OF MAN

An interesting passage in the Talmud (*Ethics of the Fathers* 5:21) presents the ages of various persons in terms of their readiness for a particular function or duty in life. Here is the passage:

The age of *five* for the study of the Bible; then *ten* for the study of the Mishnah. The age of *thirteen* for being responsible for the commandments; the age of *fifteen* for the study of Talmud. *Eighteen* for marriage; *twenty* for earning a living; *thirty* for power; *forty* for understanding; *fifty* for giving advice; *sixty* for old age; *seventy* for gray hairs; and *eighty* for special strength; *ninety* for bowed back; *one hundred*—it is as if he had died and passed away. (*Ethics of the Fathers* 5:21)

NUMBERS RELATED TO JEWISH HOLY DAYS

The Sabbath

1. The Sabbath lasts *one* day.
2. There are *two* challah (egg bread, often braided) loaves of bread used on the Sabbath.
3. There are *three* meals associated with the Sabbath.

4. *Three* stars must appear in the sky before the Sabbath ends.

5. The *fourth* commandment orders us to observe the Sabbath.

6. The Sabbath is considered the *seventh* day of the week.

The Days of Awe—
Rosh Hashanah and Yom Kippur

1. Rosh Hashanah always begins on the *first* day of the Hebrew month of Tishri.

2. *Two* days of Rosh Hashanah are observed, and *one* day of Yom Kippur.

3. There are *three* shofar blasts. They are the *tekiah* (*one* note), the *shevarim* (*three* notes), and the *teruah* (*nine* short notes).

4. The Musaf Additional Service consists of *three* sections: kingship verses, shofar verses, and remembrance verses.

5. There are *five* services that make up the total service on the Day of Atonement.

6. During the High Holidays, we observe *ten* days of repentance.

7. Yom Kippur falls on the *tenth* of the Hebrew month of Tishri.

8. It is customary for Jews to hear a total of *one hundred* calls of the ram's horn on Rosh Hashanah.

Sukkot and Simchat Torah

1. Sukkot is one of the *three* so-called pilgrimage Festivals.

2. We use *four* species on Sukkot.

3. There are *four* intermediate days of Sukkot.

4. Sukkot begins on the *fifteenth* of Tishri.

5. *Seven* circuits (*hakafot*) are made around the synagogue sanctuary on Simchat Torah.

Chanukah

1. When you play the dreidel game, if your dreidel lands on the letter *shin,* you must add more; if it falls on *nun,* you receive *0 percent;* if it lands on *hay,* you receive *half;* and if it lands on *gimel,* you receive *100 percent.*
2. There is *one shamash* (helper candle used to light the others) on the chanukiah.
3. On the first night of Chanukah, we recite *three* blessings.
4. Mattathias had *five* sons.
5. Channah had *seven* sons.
6. There are *eight* days for the Festival of Chanukah.
7. You need *forty-four* candles to light the chanukiah all the days of Chanukah.
8. Chanukah begins on the *twenty-fifth* of Kislev.

Purim

1. Purim lasts but *one* day.
2. *Mishloach manot* (food baskets) must be sent to at least *two* people.
3. Esther fasted for *three* days.
4. A hamantaschen has *three* sides.
5. Haman had *ten* sons.
6. Purim falls on the *fourteenth* of Adar.
7. Shushan Purim is on the *fifteenth* of Adar.
8. Ahasuerus ruled over *one hundred twenty-seven* provinces.
9. Haman promised the king *ten thousand* shekels for the royal treasury after the Jews were killed.

Passover

1. Passover is celebrated in the month of Nisan, the *first* month of the year.

2. There are *two* seder nights for Jews living in the Diaspora.
3. Passover falls on the *fourteenth* of Nisan.
4. *Seven* weeks is the period required for the counting of the omer.
5. Passover lasts *eight* days in the Diaspora and *seven* days in Israel.
6. There are *fifteen* parts in the seder service.
7. The *ten* plagues preceded the Israelites' Exodus from Egypt.
8. The Israelites wandered in the desert for *forty* years.
9. When Jacob and his family settled in Egypt, they totaled *seventy* souls.
10. When the Israelites left Egypt, they had *six hundred thousand* men of fighting age.

Israel Independence Day

1. The area of the State of Israel, as of May 14, 1948, was about *one-eighth* of what it was in biblical times.
2. Israel Independence Day lasts *one* day.
3. A *three-day* hike takes place just before Israel Independence Day.
4. Israel Independence Day occurs on the *fifth* of Iyar.

Lag B'Omer

1. Lag B'Omer took place during the *second* war with Rome.
2. Lag B'Omer occurs on the *eighteenth* of Iyar.
3. The words *Lag B'Omer* mean the *thirty-third* day of the counting of the omer.
4. Rabbi Akiba was *forty* years old when he first began to study the Torah.
5. The omer is counted for *forty-nine* days.

6. Rabbi Simeon bar Yochai hid in a cave for *thirteen* years.

Shavuot

1. Shavuot lasts *two* days.
2. Shavuot occurs on the *sixth* of Sivan.
3. Shavuot occurs on the *fiftieth* day after the *seven* weeks of the counting of the omer.
4. There are *six hundred thirteen* commandments in the Torah.

Jewish Fast Days

1. All Jewish fasts last *one* day or less.
2. The Fast of the Firstborn comes in Nisan, the *first* month of the year.
3. The *Second* Temple was destroyed on the *ninth* of Av, in the year *70* C.E.
4. The *three* Sabbaths of Rebuke come before the Fast of Av.
5. There are *three* weeks between the Fast of Tammuz and the Fast of Av.
6. The Fast of Gedaliah comes on the *third* of Tishri.
7. Av is the *fifth* month of the year.
8. There are *seven* Sabbaths of Consolation following the Fast of Av.
9. Tishri is the *seventh* month of the year, when the Fast of Gedaliah and the Fast of Yom Kippur take place.
10. The Fast of Av is on the *ninth* of that month.
11. The Fast of Tevet is on the *tenth* of that month.
12. Yom Kippur occurs on the *tenth* of Tishri.
13. The Fast of Esther falls on the *thirteenth* of the month of Adar.
14. The Fast of the Firstborn falls on the *fourteenth* day of Nisan.

15. The Fast of Tammuz falls on the *seventeenth* day of
    that month.

Rosh Chodesh (New Month)

1. The *first* of every month is Rosh Chodesh.
2. Sometimes Rosh Chodesh is observed for *two* days.
3. Some Hebrew months have *twenty-nine* days, whereas
   in others there are *thirty* days.

BIBLICAL WEIGHTS
AND MEASURES

From the earliest period in their history, the Israelites were aware of the need for an accurate system of weights and measures. We learn from the Book of Leviticus (19:35–36): "You shall not falsify measures of length, weight or capacity. You shall have an honest balance." A similar idea is found in the Book of Deuteronomy (25:13–16): "You shall not have in your pouch alternate weights, larger and smaller. You shall not have in your house alternate measures, a larger and a smaller. You must have completely accurate weights and completely honest measures." The Jewish prophets, too, cautioned against the use of inaccurate measures (Amos 8:5:) "If only the new moon were over, so that we could sell grain, the Sabbath, so that we could offer wheat for sale, using an *ephah* that is too small, and a shekel that is too big, tilting a dishonest scale, and selling grain refuse as grain!"

An accepted system of weights for buying and selling, building and measuring was based early on common physical phenomena such as the palm of the hand, length of the arm, a day's journey, seeds of grain, and so forth.

Biblical weights and measures were, in large part, based on the weights and measures that were accepted by the ancient peoples and retain the names by which they were known. In biblical measurement, the custom was to distinguish between natural measures (i.e., in reference to parts of the human anatomy) and more fixed measurements established by reckoning. Today, it is difficult to accurately establish the absolute values of the measures because as early as the days of the Second Temple in Jerusalem, the biblical measures were not precisely known. Any modern-day attempt to determine the exact amount of a biblical measurement is done on the basis of archaeological findings.

LINEAR MEASURE

Units of biblical length are generally derived from the average measures of the length of human limbs. Interestingly enough, the names of measurements based on limbs are often used in language today.

In the early biblical period, the custom was to measure with the limbs themselves. For example, in Deuteronomy 3:11, the standard cubit was the part of the arm from the elbow to the tip of the middle finger, and the span was the distance between the tip of the little finger and the tip of the thumb with the fingers spread. A handbreadth was the width of four fingers, and a fingerbreadth was measured according to the width of the finger.

Large biblical measures were based on primitive estimates such as the range of the bowshot (Genesis 21:16); in other words, distance that a bow is able to shoot an arrow. The Bible also used the expression "a short distance" (Genesis 35:16), which appears to mean a journey of approximately two hours. Greater distances are measured in terms of a day's journey (Genesis 30:36).

The following is a cross-section of biblical implements used for measuring small units of length.

1. Thread (Jeremiah 52:21): "As for the columns, each was eighteen cubits high and the *thread* twelve cubits in circumference; it was hollow, and the metal was four fingers thick."

2. Rope (Amos 7:17): "But this I swear, is what God said: Your wife shall play the harlot in the town, your sons and daughters shall fall by the sword, and your land shall be divided up with *rope*."

3. Measuring line (Jeremiah 31:38): "See, a time is coming, says God, when the city shall be rebuilt for God from the Tower of Chananel to the Corner Gate; and the *measuring line* shall go straight out to the Gareb Hill, and then toward Goah."

4. Measuring rod (Ezekiel 40:3): "In his hand were a cord of linen and a *measuring rod*."

Five small units of length are mentioned in the Bible. Their exact length is not explicit, but their interrelations are generally established. The units are: "reed," "cubit,", "span," handbreadth," and "fingerbreadth." The cubit was by far the most important small biblical linear measure.

It seems that there were two values for the cubit in two different periods. The "short cubit" is implied in 2 Chronicles 3:3: "These were the dimensions that King Solomon established for building the House of God: its length in cubits, by the former measure, was sixty and its breadth was twenty." The cubit in this description was six handbreadths. In the description of the future sanctuary in the Book of Ezekiel (40:5), reference is made to the longer royal cubit that was then in use: "Along the outside of the Temple area ran a wall on every side. The rod that the man held was six cubits long, plus one handbreadth for each cubit." The cubit in this description contained seven handbreadths. The exact length of the biblical cubit is not known, but estimates range from about nineteen to twenty-three inches.

MEASUREMENTS OF BIBLICAL VOLUME

Similar to linear measures, the human limbs were used initially to measure volume. Small biblical units of volume included: *handful* (Leviticus 2:2), which is the measure of the grasp of three fingers; *chofen* (Exodus 9:8), which is the entire palm of the hand; and *chofnayin,* which is two handfuls. Agricultural receptacles for grain were also used as measures and included the omer, which was a bundle of ears of corn, and a "skin jar" (1 Samuel 1:24), which held a certain quantity of wine.

The following is a summary of ten biblical units of volume.

1. *Chomer* (Leviticus 27:16): "If anyone consecrates to the Lord any land that he holds, its assessment shall be in accordance with its seed requirement: fifty shekels of silver to a *chomer* of barley seed."

2. *Kor* and *Bath* (Ezekiel 45:14): "While the due from the oil, the oil being measured by the *bath,* shall be one-tenth of a *bath* from every *kor.*"

3. *Letech* (Hosea 3:2): "Then I hired her for fifteen shekels of silver, a *chomer* of barley, a *letech* of barley . . ."

4. *Ephah* (Exodus 16:36): "The omer is a tenth of an *ephah.*"

5. *Se'ah* (Genesis 18:6): "Abraham hastened to the tent of Sarah, and said, 'Quick, three *seahs* of choice flour!' "

6. *Hin* (Exodus 29:40): "There shall be a tenth of a measure of choice flour with a quarter of a *hin* of beaten oil mixed in."

7. *Omer* (Exodus 16:16): "Gather as much of it as each of you requires to eat, an *omer* to a person for as many of you as there are."

8. *Issaron* (Leviticus 14:21): "If, however, he is poor and his means are insufficient, he shall take one male lamb for a guilt offering, to be elevated in expiation for him, one-tenth *issaron* of choice flour with oil mixed in for a meal offering, and a log of oil."

9. *Kav* (1 Kings 6:25): "There was a great famine in Samaria, and the siege continued until a donkey's head sold for eighty shekels of silver and a quarter of a *kav* of dove's dung."

10. *Log* (Leviticus 14:10): "On the eighth day he shall take two male lambs without blemish, one ewe lamb in its first year without blemish, three-tenths of a measure of choice flour with oil mixed in for a meal offering, and one *log* of oil."

The basic method of determining the values of these measures was to measure the volume of vessels found in archaeological digs that had the volume capacity marked on them. According to the calculations of W. F. Albright

(*The Archaeology of Palestine,* 1960), the royal bath had a capacity of 22 liters. Thus, the scale of measures of volume based on this calculation would be as follows:

Chomer-kor	220 liters
Letech	110 liters
Ephah-bath	22 liters
Se'ah	7.3 liters
Hin	3.6 liters
Omer-issaron	2.2 liters
Kav	1.2 liters
Log	0.3 liters

BIBLICAL MEASURE OF AREA

The basic area of biblical measurement of area was the *tzemed* (1 Samuel 14:14), which refers to the area of land that a pair of oxen could plow in a single day's work. A second system of measuring area was based upon the quantity of seeds sown in it. For example, in Leviticus 27:16 it states: "If anyone consecrates to God any land that he holds, its assessment shall be in accordance with its seed requirement."

With regard to its description of biblical rectangular area, the Bible uses a more exact measurement system, usually noting the length and width of the rectangular area in cubits or parts of cubits and adding the adjective "square." For example, in Exodus 27:1 it states: "You shall make the altar of acacia wood, five cubits long and five cubits wide; the altar is to be a *square* and three cubits high."

BIBLICAL UNITS OF WEIGHT

The verb *shakal,* meaning "to weigh," is shared by all peoples of the Semitic languages. The majority of weights were made of stone, thus the Bible usually refers to weights as *stones.*

Seven major weights are mentioned in the Bible: *talent, shekel, beka, gerah, pim,* and *kesitah.* The talent was the largest unit of biblical weight. The relationship between the talent and the shekel becomes apparent in verses 25–26 of Exodus 38: "The silver of those of the community who were recorded came to 100 talents and 1,775 shekels by sanctuary weight: a half-shekel a head, half a shekel by the sanctuary weight, for each one who was entered in the records, from the age of twenty years up, 603,550 men." The half-shekel brought by 603,550 men amounted to 100 talents and 1,775 shekels. Thus, these calculations can be made between the shekel and the talent:

    603,550 half-shekels = 300,000 + 1,775 shekels
    300,000 shekels = 100 talents
    3,000 shekels = 1 talent

The shekel is the most basic weight, and its name in Hebrew means "weight." According to Exodus 30: 13, the value of a *gerah* was one-twentieth part of a shekel. The *mina* (Ezekiel 45:12) designates a weight of approximately fifty to sixty shekels.

The *beka,* mentioned in Genesis 24:22 and Exodus 38:26, has been determined to be one-half a shekel.

If one measures a *mina* as fifty shekels, the following table may be established:

	talent	mina	shekel	beka	gerah
talent	1				
mina	60	1			
shekel	3,000	50	1		
beka	6,000	100	2	1	
gerah	60,000	1000	20	10	1

Also mentioned in the Bible is the *peres* (Daniel 5:25,28). Some biblical scholars have suggested that the *peres* is the equivalent of half a *mina*.

UNITS OF TIME

The following are some of the units of time mentioned in the Bible.

1. Jubilee (Leviticus 25:9ff.): Refers to the fiftieth year. The Bible ordained a rest from agricultural work in ancient Israel once every seven years. Any crops grown in the seventh year became communal property. The year following seven fallow years, that is, the fiftieth year, was called the Jubilee Year. At this time, cultivation was prohibited, slaves were freed, and land purchases since the previous Jubilee reverted to their original owners.

2. *Shemitta,* or Sabbatical Year: The Bible ordained a rest from agricultural work in Israel once every seven years (Leviticus 25:3ff.). Any crops grown in the seventh year were to become communal property, and slaves were allowed to go free.

3. *Shana:* A period of one year.

4. *Chodesh:* A period of one month.

5. *Shabbat:* The seventh day of the week (known as the Sabbath); a blessed day of rest.

RABBINIC WEIGHTS
AND MEASURES

Apart from the standard units of measurement, which have fixed mutual relationships, there are a great many units of measurement of biblical origin found in rabbinic literature. Sometimes these units of measurement are related to the standard units of measurement, while other times they are based on measurements taken from natural objects and utensils of that time.

UNITS OF LENGTH

The following units of length are found throughout rabbinic writings:

1. *Etzba:* A fingerbreadth or handbreadth. This is generally the smallest measure of length used in rabbinic writings. Its length in real numbers ranges from 2 to 2.5 centimeters.
2. *Tefach:* A handbreadth (i.e., the width of a clenched fist). One *tefach* is equal to four fingerbreadths.
3. *Amah:* One cubit (approximately twenty-three inches).

4. *Mil:* The talmudic "mile," which got its name from the Roman mile. One *mil* was equivalent to approximately 1,050 yards.
5. *Parsa:* A Persian mile. There are four *mils* in one *parsa.*
6. *Seet:* The distance between the index finger and the middle finger, when held as far apart as possible.
7. *Zeret:* The little finger span (i.e., the distance between the thumb and the end of one's little finger).
8. *Kaneh:* A reed, generally established as equivalent to six cubits.

UNITS OF AREA

The following is a summary of the major rabbinic units of area measurement:

1. *Etzba meru'ba'at:* This is a square handbreadth, used to measure small pieces of fabric (approximately .62 square inches).
2. *Tefach meruba:* A square handbreadth, used for measuring larger pieces of fabric (approximately 64 square centimeters).
3. *Amah meru'ba'at:* A square cubit (approximately 2,300 square centimeters).
4. *Beyt rovah:* The minimum amount of space required in order to sow one quarter of a *kav* of produce (approximately 24 square meters).
5. *Beyt kav:* The minimum amount of space required in order to sow one *kav* of produce (approximately 96 square meters).
6. *Beyt se'ah:* The minimum amount of space required in order to sow one *se'ah* of produce (approximately 576 square meters).

7. *Beyt Kor:* The minimum amount of space required in order to sow one *kor* (approximately 17,280 square meters).
8. *Se'arot:* Hairbreadths, or the space between two adjacent hairs (approximately 9 square millimeters).
9. *Greese:* A bean's area (i.e., 36 hairbreadths).

UNITS OF VOLUME

Various units of volume in the Bible found their way into rabbinic writings without including any clear way to convert them to standard talmudic units. Here is a summary of the measurements of volume found in the Talmud.

Dry Measures

1. *Baytza:* The bulk of an average egg (approximate volume of 58 cubic centimeters). This is the smallest dry measure of volume used. It was the equivalent of 1/24 of a *kav.*
2. *Uchla:* The equivalent of 1⅕ eggs, or 1/20 of a *kav.*
3. *Tomen:* ⅛ of a *kav,* or the equivalent of 3 eggs.
4. *Rova:* ¼ of a *kav,* or the equivalent of 6 eggs.
5. *Kav:* ⅙ of a *se'ah,* or 24 eggs.
6. *Tarkav:* ½ a *se'ah,* or the equivalent of 72 eggs.
7. *Se'ah:* 1/30 of a *kor,* or 144 eggs.
8. *Kor:* 30 *se'ah*s, or 4,320 eggs. This is the largest measure mentioned by name.

Liquid Measure

1. *Kortov:* 1/64 of a *log,* or 3/32 of an egg.
2. *Revi'it:* ¼ of a *log,* or 1½ eggs.
3. *Log:* 6 eggs; this is the basic unit of liquid measurement in rabbinic writings.

4. *Hin:* 12 *log*s, or 72 eggs.
5. *Arba'im se'ah:* 40 *se'ah*s, or the equivalent of 5,760 eggs.

OTHER UNITS OF MEASURE FOUND IN RABBINIC WRITINGS

In addition to the measurements previously listed, there are several others that are based on objects found in nature, particularly vegetables and fruits. Among them are:

1. *K'zayit:* an olive's size. This measurement is the amount of water that is displaced by an olive.
2. *Kotevet:* the volume of a large date.
3. *Grogeret:* the volume of a dry fig.
4. *Ka'adasha:* the volume of a lentil.
5. *Se'orah:* the volume of a barley corn.
6. *Pole halavan:* the volume of a white bean.

COINS

Many types of currency are mentioned in the Talmud. Here are some of those types that appear with more frequency.

1. *Perutah:* A copper coin, the smallest unit of rabbinic currency. In Jewish law, it was defined as the value of half a barleycorn weight of pure silver. Today it would approximate one U.S. cent.
2. *Kontirunk:* A coin worth 2 *perutah*s.
3. *Meseemas:* A coin worth 4 *perutah*s.
4. *Isar:* A coin worth 8 *perutah*s.
5. *Pundeyon:* A coin worth 16 *perutah*s.

6. *Ma'ah:* A small silver coin worth 32 *perutah*s.
7. *Dinar* or *Zuz:* A silver coin worth 6 *ma'ah*s.
8. *Shekel:* A coin worth 2 *dinar*s.
9. *Selah:* A coin worth 4 *dinar*s.
10. *Dinar zahav:* A gold coin worth 25 *dinar*s.
11. *Maneh:* A coin worth 100 *dinar*s.
12. *Maneh shel kodesh:* A coin worth 200 silver *dinar*s.
13. *Ikar:* A coin worth 60 *maneh*s.
14. *Kikar shel kodesh:* A coin worth 3,000 *selah*s.

WEIGHTS

Units of talmudic weight are closely related to talmudic units of currency, since the factor in determining coin values in rabbinic times related directly to the amount of precious metal in the coin. Here is a summary of talmudic weights:

1. *Kikar:* Weight of a silver *kikar* (approximately 27 kilograms).
2. *Maneh:* One-sixtieth of a *kikar* (approximately 450 grams, or the equivalent of one U.S. pound).
3. *Tartimar:* Half a *maneh*.
4. *Selah:* Four *dinar*s.
5. *Shekel:* Equivalent of two *dinar*s.
6. *Dinar:* The equivalent of one hundredth of a *liktra*.

THE POWER OF NUMBERS IN JEWISH SUPERSTITION

The power of numbers was a favorite subject of speculation in the ancient world and later in the world of mysticism. The occult potency of numbers was recognized, and these numbers were given an honored place in Jewish superstition. Medieval charms and magical recipes reflected this attitude. For example, the Talmud (*Shabbat* 66b) observed that incantations that are not repeated for the prescribed number of times must then be said forty-one times. However, repetition may destroy the power of the spell if the number associated with the repetition was incorrectly selected.

The common superstition that there is good fortune in odd numbers found its Jewish version in the talmudic belief that even numbers are both unlucky and dangerous.

The following are examples of the use of numbers in Jewish superstition.

THE NUMBER TWO

1. One should not attempt to do *two* things at a time or repeat an action, such as taking fire twice from a hearth, when there is an invalid in the house.

2. An unhappy fate was foreseen for any *two* couples who were married on the same day.

3. To marry off *two* children at one time or *two* sisters or brothers in one week, or indeed, to celebrate any *two* weddings within a week, was to invite trouble.

4. Tuesday was a good day for a wedding, because in Genesis it says of Tuesday "and it was good" *twice,* while of the other days this phrase is mentioned only *once.*

5. One should not visit the same grave *twice* in one day.

THE NUMBER THREE

1. Actions and incantations were to be performed *three* hours before sunrise, *three* days before the new moon, or *three* days in succession.

2. Diviners could obtain answers to only *three* questions at one time.

3. To avert the evil eye, spit *three* times on your fingertips and each time make a quick movement in the air with your hand.

4. Because evil spirits prey on the souls of little boys, boys' hair is allowed to grow until they are *three* years old so that they will be indistinguishable from little girls, who are disregarded by the spirits.

THE NUMBER FIVE

1. The *five*-finger hand is used to banish the evil eye. If one spouse gives the evil eye to the other, the other

spouse need only open his or her hand and say *chamesh* (''five''), and the evil eye will be removed.

THE NUMBER SEVEN

1. The bride or groom circles the other under the wedding canopy *seven* times because a closed circle can repel evil demons.

2. To cure a fever, take *seven* prickles from *seven* palm trees, *seven* chips from *seven* beams, *seven* nails from *seven* bridges, *seven* ashes from *seven* ovens, *seven* scoops of earth from *seven* door sockets, *seven* pieces of pitch from *seven* ships, *seven* handfuls of cumin and *seven* hairs from the beard of an old dog, and tie them to the neck hole of the shirt with a twisted cord. (Talmud *Shevuot* 15b)

OTHER NUMBERS

1. To hide good fortune from the evil eye, one avoids mentioning the date of one's birthday or exact age. If a person does mention his age, to protect himself, he adds ''until *120*'' (the age when Moses died).

2. Enumerating people or wealth can provoke the evil eye. Thus, the proper counting of people is ''not *one,* not *two,* not *three.*''

3. When a boy is born, bring *ten* people to recite the *Shema Yisrael* prayer every evening of the first week in order to ward evil demons from the room.

4. A dying child may be released from death's grasp if nominally sold by his parents for *one* shekel.

5. It is luck to be the *tenth* in a minyan.

6. To make a sick child well, multiply the age of the child by the number *eighteen* and give that amount of money to charity.

7. After a funeral, the homeward procession should stop *seven* times in order to confuse and shake off the evil spirits that follow.

8. Demons have a special affinity for the number *nine:* they congregate in groups of *nine* and in nut trees that have *nine* leaves to the branch. Moreover, incantations must be repeated *nine* times; if one has seen a demon he must not mentioned it to anyone for *nine* days; and cures are effected with *nine* kinds of herbs and are successful in *nine* days.

Interesting Numbers and the Jewish Calendar

The Jewish calendar, which is based on the moon's phases, has twelve months and 354 days. Each month is either twenty or thirty days in length. In a leap year, which occurs seven times in a nineteen-year cycle, an extra month of the calendar, Adar II, is added.

Here is a summary of the Hebrew months of the Jewish year, including the important numbers in each of the months.

NISAN (THIRTY DAYS)

1. On the eve of the fifteenth of Nisan, the Israelites prepared to leave Egypt.
2. Miriam, sister of Moses, died on the tenth of Nisan.
3. Once every twenty-eight years, in the month of Nisan, we say a blessing for the sun.

IYAR (TWENTY-NINE DAYS)

1. King Solomon built the Temple on the first of Iyar.
2. On the fifth of Iyar, in the Hebrew year 5708, the State of Israel was born.
3. Lag B'omer is always on the eighteenth of Iyar.

4. On the twenty-eighth of Iyar, in the year 5727, the city of Jerusalem was reunited.

SIVAN (THIRTY DAYS)

1. This is the third month of the Jewish calendar.
2. On the sixth of Sivan, Moses received the Ten Commandments.
3. King David was born on the sixth of Sivan and died seventy years later on the same date.

TAMMUZ (TWENTY-NINE DAYS)

1. Tammuz is the fourth month of the year and the first month of the summer.
2. On the third of Tammuz, the Jews fought a battle against the Amorites.
3. Moses came down from Mount Sinai on the seventeenth of Tammuz.
4. Noah sent a dove out of the ark on the seventeenth of Tammuz.

AV (THIRTY DAYS)

1. Av is the fifth of the Hebrew months.
2. Aaron, brother of Moses, died on the first of Av.
3. Both Jerusalem Temples were destroyed on the ninth of Av.
4. According to tradition, after the Israelites had wandered for forty years in the desert on the fifteenth of Av, God forgave them for the sin of the spies.

ELUL (TWENTY-NINE DAYS)

1. Elul is the sixth month of the Jewish year.

2. The ten spies died on the seventeenth of Elul.

TISHRI (THIRTY DAYS)

1. The first and second of Tishri are Rosh Hashanah, the beginning of the year.
2. Yom Kippur is the tenth of Tishri.
3. The festival of Sukkot begins on the fifteenth of Tishri.

CHESHVAN (TWENTY-NINE OR THIRTY DAYS)

1. Cheshvan is the eighth month of the Jewish year.
2. The flood in the time of Noah began on the seventeenth of Cheshvan.
3. Noah came out of the ark on the twenty-eighth of Cheshvan.
4. Rachel, the Jewish matriarch, died on the fourteenth of Cheshvan.

KISLEV (TWENTY-NINE OR THIRTY DAYS)

1. Kislev is the ninth of the Jewish months.
2. On the twenty-fifth of Kislev the Jews finished building the tabernacle in the desert.
3. Chanukah is celebrated on the twenty-fifth of Kislev.

TEVET (TWENTY-NINE DAYS)

1. Tevet is the tenth month of the year. It always begins on the sixth or seventh day of Chanukah.
2. On the eighth of Tevet, King Ptolemy of Egypt forced seventy-two Jewish sages to translate the Torah into Greek.

3. On the tenth of Tevet (Fast of Tevet), the Babylonian king attacked the city of Jerusalem.
4. Ezra and Nehemiah died on the ninth of Tevet.

SHEVAT (THIRTY DAYS)

1. Shevat is the eleventh month of the Jewish year.
2. On the first of Shevat in the fortieth year in the desert, Moses began to review all of the Torah with the Israelites.
3. The fifteenth of Shevat is Jewish Arbor Day, called Tu Beshevat.

ADAR (TWENTY-NINE DAYS)

1. The fourteenth of Adar commemorates the festival of Purim.
2. Moses was born and died on the seventh of Adar.

HEBREW CALENDAR NUMERICAL MISCELLANY

The first day of Passover is always the same day of the week as the ninth of Av.

The second day of Passover is always the same day of the week as Shavuot.

The third day of Passover is always the same day of the week as Rosh Hashanah.

The fourth day of Passover is always the same day of the week as Simchat Torah.

The fifth day of Passover is always the same day of the week as Yom Kippur.

The sixth day of Passover is always the same day of the week as Purim.

NUMEROLOGY AND
THE STATE OF ISRAEL

The following is a summary of some of the numerical demographic and geographic facts related to the State of Israel.

Length of the state: 280 miles
Width at widest point: 85 miles
Total area enclosed by boundaries and cease-fire lines: 10,840 square miles

Cities with more than 100,000 people:
Bat Yam, 133,000
Beersheba, 115,000
B'nai Brak, 112,000
Haifa, 224,000
Holon, 148,000
Jerusalem, 504,000
Netanya, 120,000
Petach Tikvah, 135,000
Ramat Gan, 116,000
Rishon LeZion, 129,000
Tel Aviv-Jaffa, 322,000

Major mountains:
Mount Carmel in Haifa, 1,792 feet
Mount Hermon in the Golan, 9,220 feet
Mount Meron, in Upper Galilee, 3,964 feet
Mount of Olives, Jerusalem, 2,739 feet
Mount Tabor, Lower Galilee, 1,930 feet

Main inland waters:
Dead Sea, lowest point on earth, 1,300 feet below sea
level.
Jordan River, 186 miles in length
Sea of Galilee, 695 feet below sea level

People of Israel:
Five million people, including the Jews (81.5 percent of
the population), Muslims, (14.4 percent of the population), Christians, (2.3 percent of the population), and
Druze and others (1.8 percent of the population).

Telephone area codes

02	Jerusalem
03	Tel Aviv, Ramat Gan, Givatayim, Ben-Gurion airport
04	Haifa, Acre, Nahariya
08	Ashod
051	Ashkelon
052	Herziliya
053	Netanya
057	Beersheba
059	Eilat

Gematriah: Interpretive Jewish Numerology

Gematriah is a method of disclosing the hidden meaning of a biblical or other text by reckoning the numerical equivalents of the letters of the Hebrew alphabet. The use of letters to correspond to numbers was known to the Babylonians and Greeks. The first known use of *gematriah* occurs in an inscription of Sargon II in the eighth century B.C.E., which states that the king built the wall of Khorsabad 16,283 cubits long to correspond with the numerical value of his name.

The word *gematriah* is derived from the Greek, either from *geometria* (from which the English word *geometry* derives) or from *gramma,* meaning "letter." In Hebrew, however, it denotes and connotes far more than mere mathematical values. *Gematriah* actually refers to exegetical, hermeneutical, and homiletical numerology or, to put it in simpler terms, the system of discovering the hidden sense or significance of a text by interpreting it through the number value of letters.

In Hebrew, there are no numerals (like the Arabic or Roman ones). Instead, each letter of the alphabet corresponds to a numerical value:

א	alef	1
ב	bet	2
ג	gimel	3
ד	dalet	4
ה	hay	5
ו	vav	6
ז	zayin	7
ח	chet	8
ט	tet	9
י	yud	10
כ	kaf	20
ל	lamed	30
מ	mem	40
נ	nun	50
ס	samech	60
ע	ayin	70
פ	pai	80
צ	tzaddi	90
ק	kuf	100
ר	resh	200
ש	shin	300
ת	tav	400
ך	final *kaf*	500
ם	final *mem*	600
ן	final *nun*	700
ף	final *pai*	800
ץ	final *tzaddi*	900

To express numbers from 11 to 19 and other numbers in the decimal system (21 to 29, 31 to 39, and so forth), the corresponding letter is added to each decimal unit. For example, 12 is *yud-bet* (10 plus two) and 25 is *kaf-hay*

(20 plus 5). The only exceptions are 15 and 16. These are written *tet-vov* (9 plus 6) and *tet-zayin* (9 plus 7), respectively, as the combination of the *yud* with the *hay* or *vav* forms God's Name and is therefore prohibited.

APPLICATION OF *GEMATRIAH* IN RABBINIC LITERATURE

The application of *gematriah* is found throughout rabbinic writings and occurs both in legal and legendary contexts. Numerical interpretation takes on a variety of different forms. Here is a summary of some of the more popular forms of numerical interpretation.

1. The numerical value of one word (equaling the sum of the numerical value of all its letters) is equal to that of another word. Here are several examples of the way in which this works.

According to Genesis 14:14, Abraham had 318 trained servants. This number equals the sum of the letters spelling the name *Eliezer.* Thus, the number 318 actually refers to Eliezer, the servant of Abraham mentioned in Genesis 15:2 (Talmud *Nedarim* 32a).

Yayin (wine) and *sod* (secret) equal each other numerically (70). This explains the saying, "When wine enters, secrets are out."

The ladder Jacob saw in his dream, reaching from heaven to earth, referred to *Sinai,* since the numerical value of *sulam* (ladder) equals 130, the same number value as that of Sinai. This means that the Torah, which was revealed at Mount Sinai, is the ladder that leads from earth to heaven.

Finally, the numerical value of the Hebrew word *echad* (one) is 13, which is equivalent to the Hebrew word for "love," *ahavah*. This indicates that the highest purpose that a person should try to attain is the love of God, Who is One.

2. A second form of talmudic *gematriah* relates to the squared number in which the letters of word are calculated according to their numerical value squared.

For example, the tetragrammaton YHWH, the four-letter Name of God, consists of the number equivalents 10, 5, 6, and 5, the sum of whose squares is 186 (i.e., 100 + 25 + 36 + 25). This is numerically equivalent to the Hebrew word *makom,* which means "place." Thus the word *makom* refers to God as the Omnipresent God (i.e., God is in every place).

3. A third form of *gematriah* interprets a word or phrase in terms of its numerical equivalent, where the number itself is significant. For example, in the Book of Genesis 12:1, the Hebrew words *lech lecha,* meaning "to go forth," have the number equivalent of 100. This alludes to the fact that Abraham was 100 years of age when his wife Sarah gave birth to their son Isaac.

In a second example (Genesis 18:18), the verse states that Abraham shall become (in Hebrew, *yihyeh*) a great nation. The number of *yihyeh* is 30, alluding to the belief that there are 30 saints in every generation who are as righteous as Abraham.

4. Another form of *gematriah* is the interpretation of a word by taking the numerical equivalent of each letter separately to signify something specific. For example, the Hebrew word *yitzchak,* meaning "Isaac,"

has the Hebrew letters *yud, tzaddi, chet,* and *kuf.* The *yud* has the number value of 10 and refers to the 10 trials to which Abraham was tested (according to rabbinic legend). The *tzaddi* has the number value of 90 and refers to the Sarah's 90 years of age when she gave birth to Isaac. The *chet* has the numerical equivalent of 8 and refers to the eighth day on which Isaac, Abraham's son, was circumcised. The *kuf* has the number value of 100 and refers to the age of Abraham when his son Isaac was born (*Bamidbar Rabbah* 18:21).

In a second example of this form of *gematriah,* the Hebrew word *tzedakah,* meaning "righteousness," has been described as a term relating to prayer. It is interpreted thusly: the Hebrew letter *tzaddi* has the number equivalent of 90, referring to the 90 amens. The Hebrew letter *dalet* refers to the four Sanctification of God prayers in the daily liturgy. The Hebrew letter *kuf* has the number value of 100, which is the exact number of blessings that rabbinic law requires a person to recite. The Hebrew letter *hay* is equal to the number 5, referring to the Five Books of Moses (*Tikunei Zohar* 19:40b).

5.   Another type of *gematriah* is "the filling" (*millui* in Hebrew). In this type of *gematriah,* the numerical value of each Hebrew letter itself is not calculated but instead the numerical values of all the letters that make up the names of the letter are calculated. For example, the Hebrew letters סיים spell *siyyim,* meaning "conclusion." The *gematriah* of the word *siyyum* using the "filling" type of *gematriah* is as follows:

Name of Letter	Revealed Initial	Hidden Remainder
סמך	ס = 60	מ = 40 + 20 = 60
יוד	י = 10	וד = 6 + 4 = 10
וו	ו = 6	ו = 6
מם	מ = 40	ם = 40

The Vilna Gaon comments that we learn that the revealed and the silent letters of the word *siyyum* are numerically identical so that at the *seudat siyyum,* the festive meal eaten at the conclusion of studying a talmudic tractate, two kinds of participants have equal status—the active partners, who have learned the tractate, and the inactive partners, who attend only the celebration.

6. Another form of *gematriah* consists of changing the letters of the alphabet according to the *atbash* system; this means that the last letter, "x," is substituted for the first, "a"; the penultimate "w," for the second, "b"; and so forth. This kind of *gematriah* first appears in the Bible: *Sheshach* (Jeremiah 25:26) corresponds to *Bavel* (Babylon).

A mnemonic that utilizes the *atbash* system helps to recall on which day of the week a Jewish holiday will fall in a given year. If, for example, one knows the first day of Passover, that person can determine on what days the other Jewish holidays fall by means of the first six couplets of the *atbash*. The first Hebrew letter of each couplet stands for the number of the day of Passover, while the second member of the couplet is the initial of the holiday that falls on that day of the week. Thus,

ת,,,,א—the first day of Passover falls on the same day of the week as תשעה באב, *the Ninth of Av;*
ש,,,,ב—the second day of Passover falls on the same day as שבועות, *Shavuot;*
ר,,,,ג—the third day of Passover falls on the same day as ראש השנה, *Rosh Hashanah;*
ק,,,,ד—the fourth day of Passover falls on the same day as קריאת התורה, *Simchat Torah* (lit. *reading of the Torah*);
צ,,,,ה—the fifth day of Passover falls on the same day as צום כפור, *Fast of Yom Kippur;*
פ,,,,ו—the sixth day of Passover falls on the same day as the precession פורים, *Purim* (*Shulchan Aruch, Orach Chaim* 428:3).

A reason for the preservation of the four-pronged *shin* ("ש") on the head *tefillin* is given by Levush. The Name of God in the tetragrammaton is contained in its *gematriah,* 300. According to the *atbash* system, the four letters of God's Name, "ה", "ו", "ה," and "י," correspond to "צ", "פ," "צ," and "מ," which equal 300.

OTHER INTERPRETATIONS USING *GEMATRIAH*

There are many other ways in which *gematriah* has been used to find hidden meaning in verses and texts. Here is a sampling of some of the fascinating ways in which the Rabbis have used *gematriah* interpretation.

1. In the merit of accepting God's laws as expressed in the Talmud, Israel shall be redeemed, as it is written, "ציון במשפט תפדה" "Zion shall be redeemed with justice, and they that return to her, with righteousness" (Isaiah 1:27). The Hebrew words "ציון במשפט תפדה,"

(*tziyyon bemishpat teepadeh*), which refer to Jerusalem, have the same *gematriah* "תלמוד ירושלמי" (Jerusalem Talmud 1076). The second half of the verse
"ושביה בצדקה," which speaks of the returnees from
Babylon, has the same *gematriah* as "תלמוד בבלי"
(Babylonian Talmud 524; Vilna Gaon, *Divray Eliyahu*). The combined *gematriah* of "תלמוד ירושלמי"
(1,076) and "תלמוד בבלי" (524) is 1,600. The Mishnah
begins with a "מ" (40), "מאימתי," and ends with a
"ם" (40), "בשלום." However, 40 is the square root of
1,600. This indicates that all talmudic teachings are
rooted in the Mishnah, and conversely, that a complete
understanding of the Mishnah requires the study of
both the Jerusalem Talmud and the Babylonian Talmud,
its counterpart. Furthermore, the fact that the Jerusalem Talmud begins with the Hebrew letter "א," while
the Babylonian Talmud ends with a "ת," also alludes to
the requirement of studying the Torah in its entirety,
from "א" to "ת."

2. Moses struck the "סלע" (rock) with his staff,
twice, and "מים" (water) came forth (Numbers 20:11).
The full spelling of the Hebrew letters of the word
"סלע" (rock) yields "סמך למד עין." If we strike the
"סלע" twice, the first time, knocking off the end letters
"ן", "ד," and "ך"; and the second time, eliminating the
initials "ע," "ל," and "ס"; we are left with the middle
letters "ממי," which rearrange to spell "מים" (water)
(*Be'er Mayim Chayim*).

3. The fringe on the corner of a prayer shawl has
been said to symbolize God's commandments. This is
alluded to in the very fabrication of the knots and
strands of a *tzitzit* (fringe), as well as the *gematriah* of

the word *tzitzit* itself. The word *tzitzit* has the numerical value of 600. On each fringe there are 8 strands and 5 double knots, which, added to 600, equal 613, the exact number of mitzvot (religious commandments) in the Bible.

4. The *gematriah* of the Hebrew word *Torah* is 611, referring to the 611 commandments transmitted to the Israelites through Moses, which, together with the first two commandments of the Decalogue (given directly by God on Mount Sinai), make up the 613 commandments in the Torah.

5. The *gematriah* of the Hebrew word "גט," meaning "divorce," is 12. It has been said that this is the reason a Jewish divorce is written with 12 lines.

6. The digital sum of the *gematriah* of each item that characterizes the Sabbath table is 7.

Item	Item	Letter Gematriah	Gematriah Sum	Digit sum
candle	נר	50 + 200	= 250	2 + 5 + 0 = 7
wine	יין	10 + 10 + 50	= 70	7 + 0 = 7
challah	חלה	8 + 30 + 5	= 43	4 + 3 = 7
fish	דג	4 + 3	= 7	= 7
meat	בשר	200 + 300 + 2	= 502	5 + 0 + 2 = 7

7. The significance of *gematriah* teachings is alluded to in *Deuteronomy.* In encouraging the Israelites to follow the Torah after his death, when they will be led by Joshua, Moses warns them "to observe and to perform all the words of this Torah ("כי לא דבר רק הוא מכם"),

for it is not an empty matter for you, rather it is your life" (Deuteronomy 32:47). The phrase "כי לא דבר רק הוא מכם," has the same number value (679) as the Hebrew word "גימטריאות" (*gematriahs*).

8. The Ten Commandments consist of the first five commandments, dealing with the relationship of man to God, and the last five commandments, which relate to man and his relationship to others. The equal significance of the two tablets can symbolically be seen in the numerical equality of the two commandments, each of which corresponds to the respective themes of the tablets: "ואהבת את ה אלהיך," "and you shall love the Lord, your God" (Deuteronomy 6:5), and "ואהבת לרעך כמוך אני ה," "and you shall love your neighbor as yourself" (Leviticus 19:18). The *gematriah* of each of these verses is the same—907 (Mishnah *Tzaddikim*).

9. The commandments of the Torah represent a duality of positive and negative commandments. There are 365 negative commandments, corresponding to the days of the earth's orbit around the sun, a process that is sustained by a Jewish person's observance of these commandments. There are 248 positive commandments, corresponding to the organs of a human body, to which their observance gives life (Talmud *Sanhedrin*, 23b).

10. The *Orach LeChaim* presents an interpretation using *gematriah* to the religious commandment of challah. The word "ערסתכם," "your kneading," can also be translated as "your cribs." From the time your children are babies in cribs, you should offer them to God through the commandments alluded to by the numerical value of the Hebrew letters of "challah"— "חלה":

"ח," eight—circumcise your son when he is eight days old (Leviticus 12:3).

"ל," thirty—redeem your firstborn son when he is thirty days old (Numbers 18:16).

"ה," five—when your son is five years old, begin to teach him Torah (*Ethics of the Fathers* 5:21).

11.   The difference between "בית" (house) (412) and "מקדש" (Temple) (444) amounts to 32, which is the numerical value of the Hebrew word "לב" (heart). This teaches us that only by putting one's heart into a *house* can it become a *sanctuary* in miniature.

12.   The Hebrew words "ברוך מרדכי" (blessed is Mordecai) have the same *gematriah* (502) as the Hebrew words "ארור המן" (cursed be Haman).

13.   There are two versions of the Ten Commandments in the Five Books of Moses. One version appears in Exodus 20:2–14, while the second version appears in Deuteronomy 5:16. The second version contains 17 more words than the first version. The *gematriah* of the Hebrew word "טוב" (good) is 17, indicating that the second version of the commandments assuaged man's fear that goodness had disappeared (*Baal HaTurim*).

14.   The Talmud condemns a "גס רוח", an arrogant person. The Hebrew word "גס" has the numerical value of 63. Thus, a scholar who exceeds the permissible extent of pride (i.e., 1/64th) puts himself into the category of an arrogant person (Maharsha on Genesis 32:11).

15.   The *gematriah* of the Hebrew word for "hand," "יד," is 14, alluding to the fact that the five fingers of a hand have 14 knuckles. When a certain task requires

more strength ("כח") than a single hand can provide, both hands are used. The *gematriah* of "כח" is 28, the number of knuckles in both hands (R. Hirsch).

16. The Hebrew letter "ם" and the Hebrew letter "ס" are alike in that both letters are closed. The numerical values of both letters stand for the two parts of the Torah: "ם" (40) for the Written Torah, which was given to Moses during his forty days and nights in heaven, and "ס" (60) for the Oral Law, which consists of 60 talmudic tractates (*Otiot R. Yitzhak*).

17. Protection is symbolized by the *gematriah* of the "ס" (60), as King Solomon states (Song of Songs 3:7): "Sixty mighty ones around about it, for the mighty ones of Israel. All gripping the sword, learned in warfare, each with his sword on his thigh."

18. The *gematriah* of the Hebrew letter "ק" is 100, which denotes the completion of the cycle of decimals (10 × 10 = 100). The number 100 is so significant that in our days, a minimum of 100 blessings need to be recited (*Midrash Alpha Beita*).

19. The letters of the Hebrew alphabet were used to create the world. This is alluded to by the *gematriah* of the first three words of the Torah, "בראשית ברא אלהים" which is the same as the *gematriah* of "אותיות ברא ככב"; with 22 letters God created His world (*Vayesapeir Moshe*).

20. The first Hebrew letters of the first six sentences of Deuteronomy 22, called the "Farewell Song of Moses," are *hai, yud, hai, shin, hai*. These letters have the number value of 345, identical with the numerical value of the name "משה," or "Moses." The inference here is that the spiritual doctrines contained

in these verses epitomize the philosophy of Moses in his farewell speech to his people.

21. There is a school of thought that posits that everything that has occurred or will ever occur is contained in the Bible. A follower of that doctrine was once asked where Prohibition in the United States was mentioned in the Bible. He replied: "Verse 9 of the tenth chapter of Leviticus says, 'Drink no wine or strong drink.' " The final Hebrew letters of the words of this line (in Hebrew, "ין רלת") have the number value of 680. Amazingly, it was in the year 680 of the fifth millennium (Hebrew year 5680), corresponding to 1920, that the Volstead Act ordering Prohibition went into effect!

22. The Book of Numbers 17:25 tells of the rebellion of Korach. It uses the term *mehri* (מרי) to describe his followers. The number value of *mehri* is 250, which is the exact total of the number of rebels who accompanied Korach (Numbers 16:2).

23. It is customary in many traditional wedding settings for each of the two escorts of the bride and groom to carry one candle as a sign of joy and honor. The two candles that accompany each member of the bridal pair are seen as particularly auspicious, for the numerical value of the Hebrew word for "candle" (*ner*) multiplied by 2 (i.e., 500) is equal to the numerical value of the phrase, "be fruitful and multiply" (*p'ru ur'vu*). Thus, the candles represent the parents' wish for their children to successfully build a family.

24. "Behold, I send an angel before you, to keep you by the way. . . . Take heed of him and do not listen to his voice . . . for My Name is in him (Exodus 23:20ff.).

Because the Name of God resides in this angel, he must be Metatron, the high-ranking angel of goodness. The numerical name of God is *Shaddai* (״שדי״) (314). Hence, the Name of God resides in the angel Metatron.

25. There are thirty-nine coils on each of the fringes of a *tallit.* The thirty-nine coils are symbolic, for they are equal to the number of books in the Jewish Bible.

26. After Jacob's dream of the ladder and angels (Genesis 28:10 ff.), he awakens and says, "God is in this place" (יש יהוה במקום הזה). The numerical value of these words is 541. The Hebrew word for Israel, *Yisrael,* also has the number value 541, thus teaching us that God promises the Land of Israel to the Jewish people.

27. In the following *gematriah* example, the total number of letters contained in the word reveals something about the word itself. Abraham (אברהם), Isaac (יצחק), and Jacob (יעקב) have a total of thirteen letters in them. Sarah (שרה), Rebekkah (רבקה), Rachel (רחל), and Leah (לאה), their wives, also have thirteen letters. This reveals a distinct design. The number thirteen is the *gematriah* of the Hebrew word for "one" (אחד), hinting that the concepts contained in Abraham, Isaac, and Jacob are found in one person, their heir, the Jewish man. This is also true for Sarah, Rebekkah, Rachel, and Leah, whose characteristics are found in their heir, the Jewish woman. Thirteen plus thirteen equals twenty-six, the numerical value of "Adonai" (יהוה), God's Holy Name.

28. Isaac Luria, the famous kabbalist, has taught that when eating bread one should dip the bread in salt three times. The reason for his teaching is that the word for God, "Adonai" (יהוה), has the number value of 26.

Three times 26 equals 78, the *gematriah* for both salt ("מלח") and bread ("לחם").

29. The first letter of the Hebrew alphabet is an *aleph,* which has the number value of 1. The *aleph* is written by combining three Hebrew letters, a *yud* (י), a *vav* (ו), and another *yud* (י), which total 26. The *gematriah* of God's Name, "Adonai" (יהוה), has the number value of 26, thus revealing through *gematriah* that God is indeed One!

30. The values of God's Names can be computed, and when these numbers are counted from the very beginning of the Torah, an insight about God is revealed. *Yah* (יה) equals 15. The 15th letter of the Torah is an *aleph,* having the number value of 1. The word for God, *Adonai,* has the number value of 26. The twenty-sixth letter of the Torah is an *aleph.* "El" (אל), another word for God, has the number value of 31. The thirty-first letter in the Torah is an *aleph. Elohim* (אלהים), another word used for God, has the number value of 86—and the eighty-sixth letter in the Torah is an *aleph.* The Hebrew letter *aleph* is placed in these locations by design, in order to teach and constantly remind us that God is One God.

31. It has been told by the Rabbis that in order to memorize something, one must repeat it 101 different times. When "remember" (זכר), which has the number value of 227, is subtracted from the Hebrew word for "forget" (שכח), which has the number value 328, the difference between remember and forget is 101!

32. Sometimes even Jewish law can be revealed using the principles of *gematriah*. The Talmud (*Nazir* 5a) states that if a man becomes a Nazirite and does not

state for how long he plans to do so, his vow will be for a minimum of 30 days, since the Bible states, "he will be a Nazir," and the Hebrew word for "he will be," *yihiyeh* (יהיה), has the numerical value of 30.

33. The sum of the Hebrew letters in the Ten Commandments, with the exception of the 7 letters in the last two Hebrew words *asher le're'echa* ("that is your neighbor's"), is 613, corresponding to the 613 commandments in the Torah. Some rabbis explained that the last 7 letters correspond to the 7 Noachian laws, which obligate not only the Jews but also "your neighbor." Others have interpreted these extra letters as referring to the 7 days of creation, thus teaching that the entire world was created on the merit of the Torah (*Numbers Rabbah* 13:15, 18:21).

34. It is customary to read the Book of Ruth on the Festival of Shavuot. This can be alluded to by the fact that the numerical value of the Hebrew letters in her name total 606, the number of precepts that Ruth accepted as a proselyte on her conversion to Judaism. These 606 commandments, when added to the 7 Noachian precepts (which were previously Ruth's responsibility), are equivalent to 613, the exact number of religious obligations in the Torah.

35. The Hebrew month of Elul, preceding the month of Tishri, when a New Jewish Year is proclaimed, has traditionally been the month to prepare the Jew for the days of repentance. The month of Elul (אלול) has the number value of 67. The Hebrew word "בינה," meaning "understanding," also has the number value of 67. This indicates that understanding is needed in order for a person to fully be able to repent.

36. There are 365 negative commands in the Bible and 248 positive ones. Thus, the Rabbis taught (Talmud *Makkot* 23b–24a):

"Moses was given 365 negative commandments that correspond to the 365 days of the year. He was given 248 positive commandments to correspond to the 248 parts of the human body. This teaches that people should be performing the commandments every day with all of their human powers."

37. It is customary on the Festival of Sukkot to spread branches of a tree for the roof of the *sukkah*. This may be deduced from the Hebrew word for "tree," *ilan,* which has the number value of 91. The word *sukkah* has the same number value!

38. In the verse "On the eighth day a solemn gathering shall be for you" (Numbers 29:35), referring to the holiday of Shemini Atzeret, the numerical value of the sum of the Hebrew word *lachem* ("for you") is 90, the same as the number value of the Hebrew word *mayim,* meaning "water." This indicates that on Shemini Atzeret the prayer for rain ought to be recited.

39. The Hebrew number equivalent of the word *lulav,* meaning "palm branch," is 68, the same as for *chacham* ("wise person") and *chayyim* ("life") Thus, the *lulav* is held in the right hand opposite one's heart, in conformity with the Bible, which states that "a wise person's heart tends toward the right hand" (Ecclesiastes 10:2). Similarly, the numerical similarity of *lulav* and *chayyim* denote that the *lulav* must be fresh and not withered.

40. The Talmud has stated that the "seal of the Almighty is Truth." The Hebrew word for "truth" is

"אמת" which is composed of the first, the middle, and
the last letters of the Hebrew alphabet. "Whatever decree bears the seal of the Lord, Truth, is immutable; for
aleph is the first, *mem* is the middle, and *tav* the last
letter of the alphabet," as it is related in the *Midrash
Genesis Rabbah* 81: "This being the Name of God,
according to Isaiah 44:6, 'I am the first, I am the middle,
there being one who shares the kingdom with Me; and I
am the last, there being none to whom I shall hand the
kingdom of the world.' "

The first two Hebrew letters of the word *emet* form
the word *em,* meaning "mother," the beginning of life.
The last two letters of the word *emet* form the word
met, meaning "death." This implies, gematrically
speaking, that the world exists only through truth. In
addition, the number value of the word *emet* is 441,
which is diminished to 9 by ignoring the zeroes (4 + 4
+ 1). This is to say that "just as the seal of God is
Truth," it represents the number 9.

Just as truth is immutable, so, too, the number 9 is
never lost. If you multiply it by any other number or
even by itself, the sum of the answer will answer be 9
(example: 9 × 9 = 81; 8 + 1 = 9; 9 × 150 = 1350; 1 +
3 + 5 = 9).

Additionally, if you add the number 9 to any number,
the answer (when reduced to simple digits with the elim-
ination of the zeroes) will always be the same as the
number to which 9 was added (examples: 9 + 175 =
184—175 = 1 + 7 + 5 = 13; 1 + 3 = 4; 184, the answer
arrived at by adding 9 + 175, is 1 + 8 + 4 = the identical
13, or 4 when reduced; 9 + 12 = 21; 12 = 1 + 2 = 3; 21,
the answer arrived at by adding 9 + 12, is identical).

One can also divide 9 only into numbers whose total is 9 (the simple digits without the zeroes). Subtract 9 from any figure and the answer will have the identical total as the number from which it was subtracted. That is to say, the number 9 never loses its identity and always remains complete and unchanged. This is because it represents *emet*—the truth, the seal of God, which is unchanging!

41. The numerical value of the letters in *haSatan* (the Satan) is 364, which is one short of the number of days in the year. Thus, Satan is given the authority to make accusations against the children of Israel on all the days of the year except on the Day of Atonement, when the Holy One, blessed be He, says to him: "You have no authority to touch them. Nevertheless, go forth and see wherein they busy themselves." Then Satan, going forth, finds all of them at fasting and prayer, dressed in white garments and cloaked like the ministering angels, and forthwith goes back in shame and confusion (*Midrash on Psalms* 27:4).

42. Some have forecasted the holiday of Chanukah in the early stories of the Bible. For example, the account of Creation describes God as creating light by stating *yehi or*—"let there be light" (Genesis 1:3). The Hebrew word *yehi* has the number value of 25. This has been interpreted to portend that on the twenty-fifth day of the month, there is to be light. Chanukah falls on the twenty-fifth of Kislev.

43. When Jacob met Esah, the Bible states that "the sun shone for him." In Hebrew, the Bible says "*vayizrach lo hashemesh*" (Genesis 32:32). The Hebrew word *lo* has the number value of 36. Now, instead of *hashemesh,*

"the sun," one can substitute *hashammash,* meaning the candle that lights the others on the Chanukiah. Thus, the verse reads that the "*shamash*" shone for the 36 comrades.

44. The last day of Chanukah is considered by some people to have a special significance in the culmination of the holiday, the day when the chanukiah burns the most brightly. It is called "*zot Chanukah,*" literally "this is Chanukah," because these are the opening words of the Torah reading. According to one tradition, *zot chanukah* means "this is the essence of Chanukah." This is connected to the role that the number 8 plays in the tradition. The number 7 is the perfect number, the number of completion. The week and Sabbath, the sabbatical years, the omer (7 × 7) all reflect the importance of the number 7. Eight is 7 + 1, namely, 1 beyond the number of completion. If 7 marks the limit of time by marking the limits of the week, then 8 is beyond time. Thus, 8 signifies the eternal. Just as the holiday of Shemini Atzeret is a special day when God asked His people to stay for one more day with Him, so the eighth day of Chanukah is the essence of Chanukah and a reminder of the light that is ever present in this world.

45. There are 613 letters in the Ten Commandments, equal to the total number of commandments (*Midrash Numbers Rabbah* 13:15).

46. The Hebrew word for "woman" (*isha*) has the same number value (342) as the Hebrew word for "honey" (*devash*).

47. One is advised (*Tanchuma Buber, Shemini* 5) that if you avoid drinking wine (in Hebrew, *yayin*) whose number value is 70, you will not be sum-

moned to appear before the 70 in the Sanhedrin (i.e., the Jewish court).

48. The *gematriah* value of the two candles carried by the two best men at a wedding is 500 (i.e., *ner* = *ner*). This is equivalent to the numerical value of God's first blessing to Adam and Eve: *p'ru ur'vu,* "be fruitful and multiply" (500).

49. Willow leaves that form part of the Hoshana Rabbah rite induce conception because the Hebrew word for willow, *aravah,* and the Hebrew word for seed, *zera,* have the same numerical value of 277.

50. The Massoretes, researchers, and rabbis of years ago, who lovingly examined and structured the Torah text, inform us that there are 5,845 verses in the Five Books of Moses. We can remember that Bible statistic by taking note of the Hebrew word *hachamah* ("החמה"), "the sun," which has the number value of 5,845. As the sun spells life for humanity, the Torah means life to Jewry.

51. The Hebrew letter *heh,* which begins Deuteronomy 32:6, is written large. According to the Tanchuma (*Haazinu* 5), the letter *hey* is the last letter of Moses' hidden signature in his song. To prove that this is so, the total numerical value of the first letters of Deuteronomy 32:1–6 is 345. The numerical value of the Hebrew word for "Moses," *Moshe,* is also 345.

52. The most powerful expression of will is love, which is an integral part of the prayer *Shema Yisrael.* The number value of *echad,* Hebrew for "one," is 13. The numerical value of *ahavah* ("love") is also 13. Thus, two people who are deeply in love become one, and there is no greater love than between God and human beings.

53. The last letter of the Hebrew word *shema* is an *ayin,* which has the number value of 70. According to the *Zohar,* the letter *ayin* represents the seventy different forces of creation. These seventy forces are manifest in the seventy nations and seventy languages, as well as the seventy descendants who accompanied Jacob to Egypt. In listening to the message of unity in the *Shema,* one brings these seventy forces into the ear and mind and unifies them with God.

54. God revealed Himself to Moses in the burning bush, and thus hinted to Moses the exact age in years when he would die. The Hebrew word for "bush" is *sneh,* which has the numerical value of 120.

FOR FURTHER READING

Bialik, Hayim Nahman, and Ravnitzky, Yehoshua Hana, eds. *The Book of Legends.* New York: Schocken, 1992.

Douglas, J. D., organizing ed. *New Bible Dictionary.* Leicester: Intervarsity Press, 1962.

Greenberg, Haaron Yaakov. *Torah Gems.* 3 vols. Tel Aviv: Yavneh Publishing House, 1992.

Hausdorff, David M. *A Book of Jewish Curiosities.* New York: Bloch Publishers, 1955.

Locks, Gutman G. *The Spice of Gematriah.* New York: Judaica Press, 1985.

Markowitz, Sidney. *Jews, Religion, History, Ethic and Culture.* Secaucus, NJ: Citadel Press, 1982.

Paul, Shalom M., and Dever, William G., eds. *Biblical Archaeology.* New York: Quadrangle/New York Times Book Company, 1974.

Plaut, Gunther, ed. *The Torah: A Modern Commentary.* New York: Union of American Hebrew Congregations, 1981.

Riedel, Eunice, Tracy, Thomas, and Moskowitz, Barbara D. *The Book of the Bible.* Toronto, Canada: Bantam Books, 1981.

Schimmel, Annemarie, *The Mystery of Numbers.* New York: Oxford University Press, 1993.

Wenger, Rliezer. *The Jewish Book of Lists and Summaries.* Vols. 1, 2. Houston, TX: B'ruach HaTorah Publications, 1979.

INDEX